# A
# Torchlight
# for
# America

# A Torchlight for America

Minister
## Louis Farrakhan

FCN Publishing Co.
Chicago

Library of Congress Catalog Card Number: 93-79288
ISBN: 0-9637642-4-1

Printed in the United States of America

First Edition

Second printing, September, 1993

# *Contents*

# ACKNOWLEDGMENTS

No human being who accomplishes anything of significance in life should use the personal pronoun "I" in reference to the accomplishment. For each one of us represents a community of persons unseen who helped to make us what we are. Therefore, the Bible uses the term "Us" in reference to God's making of man. "...Let us make man..." (Genesis 1:26) The term "We" is used in the Holy Qur'an. "And surely We created man of sounding clay, of black mud fashioned into shape." (Sura 15, Verse 26)

This work called, *"A Torchlight for America,"* is not an individual effort. Although one person's name is represented as the author, he could not have done any of this without the Guidance of Allah (God) and the Teachings of the Honorable Elijah Muhammad and the many persons who are the unseen community that has helped to make me and this book what we are.

I give the greatest thanks to Allah, Who came in the Person of Master Fard Muhammad, the Great Mahdi, and to His Servant and Apostle, the Honorable Elijah Muhammad.

I would like to give special thanks to Keith Hopps, who worked with me throughout the writing and production process.

I would like to further thank Jabril Muhammad for his assistance in editing the manuscript, and Rafi Kushmir, who designed the layout and graphics.

I also extend my appreciation for the time and thoughtful statements from those who reviewed this book.

# PREFACE

This book represents some of the guiding principles taught to us by the Honorable Elijah Muhammad. This man and his teachings have been responsible for transforming the lives of millions of black men and women, many of whom this society has rejected as incorrigible, irredeemable, irreformable, irretrievable, hopeless and lost. Yet, the Honorable Elijah Muhammad, with the Word of Allah (God), has been able to initiate the process of our salvation, redemption and resurrection, which continues to this day.

There are tens and hundreds of thousands of black people in this country who have been influenced by the teachings of the Honorable Elijah Muhammad, through my work. We come from all walks of life. Some of us are learned, some are not. Some are young and some are old. Yet we have been able, by the grace of Allah (God), to produce a community of people that is relatively free from the ills that plague the larger black community and the broad mass of the American people.

We believe that it is time for America to closely examine the Honorable Elijah Muhammad, his message and the people who have come to follow his teachings.

As America prepares to make a change, she is seen searching for new solutions to her plethora of problems. Every aspect of American society is suffering. Her economy is faltering, her public schools are failing, maintaining the health of the American people has proven too costly, crime is rampant, her sense of morality seems to have been lost, and in general the whole future of the country has become a big question.

We would like to offer the words of the Honorable Elijah Muhammad, with ourselves as an example of what those words can produce, as a "torchlight" for America.

A torchlight is anything that serves to illuminate, enlighten or guide. It also means to love someone or something that does not necessarily reciprocate love. The bearer of the torchlight is a person who imparts knowledge, truth or inspiration to others.

This book is humbly submitted as a torchlight for guiding the country out from its present condition toward a more peaceful and productive society in which mutual respect governs the relations between the diverse members of America.

I hope that you receive this torchlight with open ears and an open heart, with the aim of discovering those truths that can lay the base for developing honest remedies for the condition of America.

# CHAPTER

# 1

# AMERICA IS ON HER DEATHBED

America is clearly suffering, and from my vantage point, America lies on her deathbed in dire need of guidance and a new direction. If you examine her vital signs, you will have to agree that they show America is steadily on the decline.

The root of her suffering is basic immorality and vanity, where greed, lust and inordinate self-interest has become the way of life.

When the desire for the realization of self-interest becomes excessive, the first casualty in this struggle is "truth." The leaders in the society, in their struggle to achieve inordinate self-interests, engage in hiding the light of truth from the American people.

Without truth the American people are left paralyzed, unable to constructively address their problems.

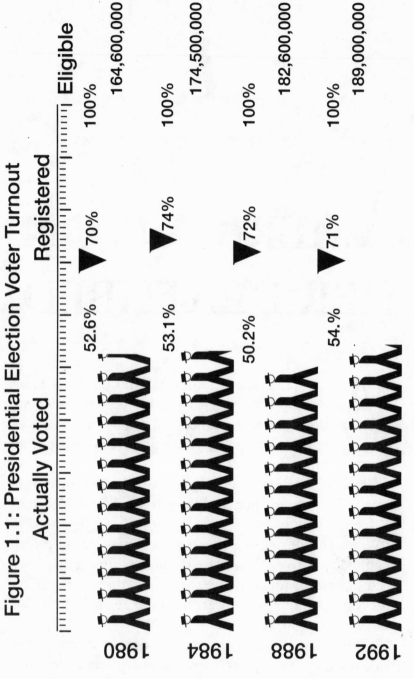

Figure 1.1: Presidential Election Voter Turnout

Source: Committee for the Study of the American Electorate

Eventually, their only response will be to react destructively because their very lives are at peril's door, and they know not why they are in this condition nor how to save themselves.

So the country could be facing revolution because, in the main, the government and leadership has hidden the truth and will not or does not have a solution for the suffering and the root problems of the people of this country.

Gross vanity, greed, lust and inordinate self-interest have divided the country along the lines of class, race and sex. We live in one country with two realities, separate and unequal: one rich, one poor; one white, one black; one predator, one prey; one skilled, one non-skilled; one slavemaster, and one slave.

Classism, racism and sexism are used to keep the people divided, and these three evils threaten to sink and destroy the entire country. America must deal effectively with these lines of division or face anarchy and revolution.

A mere 54% of those eligible to vote actually bothered to participate in the 1992 presidential election of this great country. (See Figure 1.1) This is a sign on which the wise should reflect. If the greatest political system is democracy and the right to choose the leadership, and if only half of the people are participating in this democracy, then the people are demonstrating their gross dissatisfaction with their own leadership and government. This dissatisfaction must bring about a change. The question becomes: Who will bring about the change? Who will offer solutions to the problems faced by the people and what kind of change will there be?

# Figure 1.2: What $4 Trillion Looks Like

A stack of $4 trillion
in dollar bills would
overshoot the moon
(by 35 miles)

Source: U.S. Department of the Treasury, Public Affairs Dept.;
The World Book Encyclopedia

How will you deal with a solution, a Divine solution, a torchlight, if it is not carried by someone of your own class, sex, faith, color, party or nationality? How will you deal with a solution when it comes from a source you least expect? Would you cast the solution aside, or seek to destroy the bearer of the solution? Or would you thank God for giving you an answer to your problems and your prayers?

The Bible states, *"No man, when he hath lighted a candle, putteth it in a secret place, neither under a bushel, but on a candlestick, that they which come in may see the light."* (Luke 11:33) It is the purpose of the wickedly wise to hide the truth so that people won't see a way to get themselves out of their present circumstances, so those who rule can continue to dominate and subjugate the people to feed their own lusts and greed.

I submit to you that this is a dangerous time to play with the people and their earnest desire for liberty. It's a dangerous time to play with people whose hunger and thirst is for justice and truth. Like Moses and Aaron were unto Pharaoh, I humbly state that I am here as a student and helper of the Honorable Elijah Muhammad to tell the truth. We, the followers of Elijah Muhammad, are here to demonstrate our love for our people and our concern for the worsening condition of America and its people, whether the people of America feel the need to reciprocate or not. I am here to present a torchlight that is intended to save ourselves, as well as all of America, if she will only take heed.

Let's take a quick look at the vital signs of America, from our perspective.

# Figure 1.3: Federal Budget Deficits Since 1964

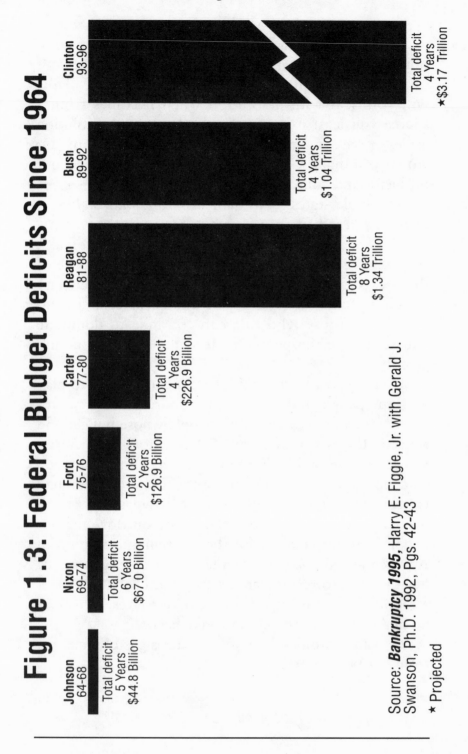

Source: *Bankruptcy 1995*, Harry E. Figgie, Jr. with Gerald J. Swanson, Ph.D. 1992, Pgs. 42-43

★ Projected

## AMERICA'S VITAL SIGNS

The health of the economy, the standard of living of the American people, our lifestyles and the development of the people are all in a state of decline. America's economy has been severely crippled for the long-term, and at present the U.S. economy is in a state of grave disrepair.

The federal debt, which is basically the cumulative sum of each year's budget deficits, is now more than $4 trillion. (See Figure 1.2) The current budget for federal spending is $1.5 trillion, but the government collects just a little over $1 trillion in taxes. This means that America is running a budget deficit of nearly $500 billion, 5 times larger than the deficit of a decade ago when Mr. Ronald Reagan became the president. So on top of the federal debt, each year America is running a deficit, and at the current rate - in just four more years - the federal debt will equal the entire gross national product of the country, which is now approximately $6 trillion.

The interest alone, in servicing the federal debt, soared to $288 billion in 1991, nearly one-third of what America collects in taxes. Now what does this mean? If the level of tax revenue remains constant, and the level of federal debt is not cut, then at the end of President Clinton's four years, the interest alone on the federal debt could eat up all of what the government collects in taxes, rendering the country bankrupt in terms of having revenue to finance the government's provision of services to the American people. In Harry E. Figgie, Jr.'s book *Bankruptcy 1995*, he forewarns this very scenario. He projects that President Clinton's budget deficits could exceed $3 trillion by the end of 1996, bringing the total federal debt to more than $7 trillion,

# Figure 1.4: Ownership of Federal Debt

| Type of Investor | As a % of Total Debt | As a % of Public Debt |
|---|---|---|
| 1. Foreign | 11.2% | 17.9% |
| 2. State & local government | 8.2% | 13.1% |
| 3. Individuals | 6.4% | 10.3% |
| 4. Commercial banks | 5.4% | 8.6% |
| 5. Insurance companies | 3.9% | 6.3% |
| 6. Corporations | 3.6% | 5.7% |
| 7. Money market funds | 1.6% | 2.6% |
| 8. Other investors* | 22.2% | 35.5% |
| Subtotal | 62.5% | |
| 9. Government Agencies | 37.5% | |
| TOTAL | 100% | 100.0% |

* Includes S&Ls, credit unions, non-profit institutions, mutual savings banks, corporate pension trust funds, dealers and brokers, certain government deposit accounts, and government sponsored agencies.

SOURCE: U.S. Dept. of Treasury (Economic Report of the President 1992, p. 396)

NOTE: Public debt is debt held by the public, both domestic and foreign publics, and does not include debt that is held by government agencies.

which would make interest payments to service the debt equal to the country's tax revenue. (See Figure 1.3)

The federal debt is financed mainly by issuing government securities, such as Treasury bills and savings bonds. So, when the government needs money, it borrows from people who can buy these securities. And who are these people? The rich and some of the middle class. So rich Americans, and those foreigners and foreign governments that can afford it, buy government securities and get paid interest from the increasing indebtedness of America. (See Figure 1.4)

Most of the government securities that are issued (about 70%) have short-term maturities. (See Figure 1.5) In other words, the securities have to be repaid in one to five years. Since the government cannot repay the debt within the short term, it is forced to refinance the debt by issuing more securities. So the rich, who can buy the securities, hold the American taxpayer in perpetual debt, as the debt is continually being refinanced. The taxpayers become the slaves to the debt held by the rich in America and the rich abroad.

About one third of the total federal debt is financed by surpluses in other government agencies and accounts, such as social security, railroad retirement insurance and pension funds.[1] This means that a check is written against the excess money in government accounts. A check is written against the accounts that were set up for the people who have worked hard all their lives so that they would have something upon retirement. Where they might have thought they would end up in their old age at least being able to survive economically, now they can't even count on that. This is because America has written checks against what it had promised to set aside for the future of its people.

# Figure 1.5: Maturity Schedule of Federal Debt *

| When Debt Matures | % of Total |
|---|---|
| within 1 year | 34.2% |
| 1-5 years | 36.3% |
| 5-10 years | 12.6% |
| 10-20 years | 4.0% |
| 20 years and over | 12.9% |
| **TOTAL** | **100%** |

Source: U. S. Dept. of Treasury (Economic Report of the President 1992, p. 395). * Based on debt held by the public.

Note: Average maturity is 6 years

So, America has seriously <u>mortgaged</u> its future. Americans cannot save or invest because taxes eat up what little disposable income the people have. These taxes are needed to cover government spending. The United States now has the lowest savings and investment rates of any of the industrialized countries. The national savings rate is just 15% of the gross national product (GNP), while Japan's is nearly 35%. Most households save nothing. In fact, most households are in debt, barely making it from paycheck to paycheck, as credit card debt is approaching $1 trillion.

Supply-side economics has **not** trickled down better wages, employment opportunities, better schools, better roads, affordable housing, safer streets, universal health care, increased small-business opportunities and all of the things that were promised by Reaganomics.

Each year the country finishes with a trade deficit of about $100 billion, so over the past decade the trade deficit has accumulated to $1 trillion, meaning America has been importing $1 trillion more in goods than it is exporting.[2]

In sum, America entered the eighties as the largest creditor nation, and now in the nineties it has become the world's largest debtor nation.[3] The American people have been made slaves to a mortgaged future and to servicing borrowed money.

The Honorable Elijah Muhammad taught us that debt is slavery. In Proverbs it reads, *"The rich ruleth over the poor, and the borrower is servant to the lender."* (Proverbs 22:7) So the same America that once enslaved is now being enslaved, through indebtedness, fulfilling the scripture that *"..as thou hast done, it shall be done unto thee..."* (Obadiah 1:15)

## Figure 1.6: Earnings of Top 4% of the Population versus the Bottom Half

**In 1989** (each symbol=1 million workers):

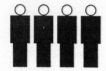 ◄ **The top 4%**
(3.8 million individuals and families) earn $452 billion in wages and salaries-the same as

**the bottom 51%**
(49.2 million individuals and families) ►

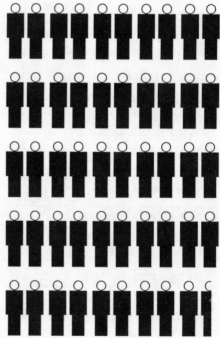

Source: Internal Revenue Service

The country is in a state of severe unemployment and poverty.  Some believe that this condition is worsening.  The cost of living has placed the American dream beyond the reach of the majority of the people.  About 10 million Americans over age 16 are jobless.[4]  This figure is continuing to climb.  Black people make up 20% of the unemployed and a large percentage of those who have dropped out of the job market or stopped looking altogether.  This proportion has been the same since the sixties, illustrating that suffering is nothing new for us and that integration and the civil rights movement have done very little toward addressing the root problem among the masses of black people.[5]

Though America's population has increased, there were more people employed in 1989 than there are today.[6]  Millions of workers have been displaced by plant closings and relocations to foreign markets, such as Mexico, where labor costs are a fraction of U.S. labor costs.  Since 1980, over 2 million manufacturing jobs have vanished in America while at the same time the adult population has risen by 11%.[7]

If you can get a job, you become one of the "working poor."  This is because many of the job openings are in low-skilled positions that pay minimum wage.  The average real wage is lower today than twenty years ago.[8]  In other words, the check you bring home today buys less than it did two decades ago.

In 1989 the top 4% of America's families and individuals earned as much as half the entire country put together.  (See Figure 1.6)  In fact, in the '80s the only people whose salaries increased were those who were already taking in over $200,000.  In other words, the rich got richer and the poor got poorer.

# Figure 1.7: Closing the Racial Income Gap

If blacks continue to gain on whites at the same rate as they have during the past 20 years, they will not achieve equality until the year 2420

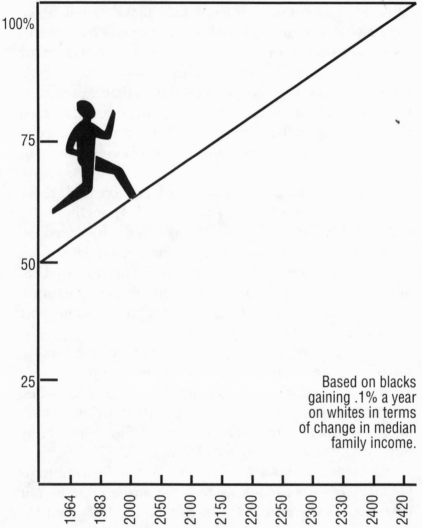

Based on blacks gaining .1% a year on whites in terms of change in median family income.

Source: Theodore Cross, *The Black Power Imperative: Racial Inequality and the Politics of Nonviolence.*

Blacks, Native Americans and Hispanics, of course, suffer more than whites from unemployment. Those who are employed make only 60% of what whites make.[9] One study shows that if we track the closing of the gap between white and black incomes, blacks might achieve income parity in the year 2420, although there is still no guarantee that the gap will be closed by then. (See Figure 1.7) That means 428 years from today we might become equal to whites in terms of income. I should think that most would agree that this is entirely too long to hope to close the gap, and entirely too unjust.

Over 30 million Americans live in poverty, and 10 million of those are black.[10] One third of the total black population lives in poverty and nearly half of all black children are growing up in poverty. We're growing up under conditions that give us a higher propensity toward disease and malnutrition, and each succeeding generation is passed into what is called a permanent underclass. Millions more of us are living on the brink of poverty, just one plant closing away from poverty's door.

Housing costs have soared to over $100,000 on average, and the cost of college education is projected to exceed $100,000 for four years by the end of the decade. If this economic condition continues, who will be able to afford decent housing and a decent education?

So as we see, the standard of living of the American people is sinking, and there is no sign of relief in sight. America is like the great Titanic that no one thought would ever go down, but she's sinking right now, for sure. Changing captains on a sinking ship will not stop the ship from sinking. We need to either get off the ship

# Figure 1.8: Age Breakout of Rape Victims

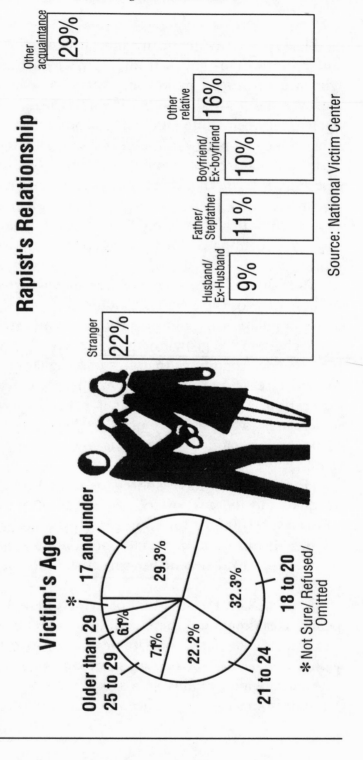

## Rapist's Relationship

Other acquaintance: 29%
Other relative: 16%
Boyfriend/Ex-boyfriend: 10%
Father/Stepfather: 11%
Husband/Ex-Husband: 9%
Stranger: 22%

## Victim's Age

17 and under: 29.3%
18 to 20: 32.3%
21 to 24: 22.2%
25 to 29: 7.1%
Older than 29: 6.1%*

* Not Sure/ Refused/ Omitted

Source: National Victim Center

that's sinking, or, if we are to remain on this ship, there will have to be a total reconstruction of the ship. You can't just do patchwork on a ship that's going under. The problem is in getting the ship to dry dock before it sinks.

Living in America's cities has become like living in a war zone. Street crime has become the norm throughout America's cities and even in many of the suburbs. It's difficult to walk the streets in America without the fear of being assaulted or actually being assaulted. It's difficult to drive your car without the threat of being carjacked. Someone may kill you over a Bulls' jacket, or stick you up over a gold chain or Air Jordan shoes.

Dope has become the major employer in urban communities. The dope industry is greater than a $300 billion industry, three times the size of General Motors, the No. 1 company of the Fortune 500.[11] Drugs are the primary cause of street violence. Over a million suspected drug violators were arrested last year.[12]

According to the National Victim Center, nearly three quarters of a million women and girls were raped last year. A third of these rapes takes place among children. (See Figure 1.8) On top of this, another 2 million women are victims of wife beating or domestic violence. At the root of most arguments in the home is money, or the lack of it. Yet many politicians, who have shown no compassion for unemployment and the poor, say they support promoting family values.

There are over one million inmates in America's jails and prisons, nearly half of whom are black, making America the world's leader in incarceration rates.[13] The Justice Department estimates that the annual incidence of crime is about 6% of households.

# Figure 1.9: International Health & Health-Care Spending Indicators

| | Life Expectancy at Birth (years) Male | Life Expectancy at Birth (years) Female | Infant Mortality (per 1,000 live births) | Health Spending as Percent of GDP | Doctors per 10,000 Population |
|---|---|---|---|---|---|
| Japan | 75.9 | 81.8 | 4.6 | 6.7 | 16 |
| Germany | 71.8 ★ | 78.4 ★ | 7.5 | 8.2 | 30 |
| United States | 71.5 | 78.5 | 9.7 | 11.8 | 23 |
| United Kingdom | 72.4 ★ | 78.1 ★ | 8.4 | 5.8 | 14 |
| France | 72.4 | 80.6 | 7.5 | 8.7 | 30 |
| Canada | 73.0 ★ | 79.8 ★ | 7.2 ★ | 8.7 | 22 |
| Holland | 73.7 | 80.0 | 6.8 | 8.3 | 24 |

Source: Organization for Economic Cooperation and Development. ★ Data for 1985 and 1986.

Even larger than the drug industry and street crime, in terms of dollars, is white-collar crime. The Savings & Loan (S&L) bailout alone is half a trillion of the taxpayers' dollars.[14] Michael Milken and Ivan Boesky beat the economy out of billions of dollars with their junk-bond scheme that bankrupted the S&Ls. This kind of crime has eroded public confidence and placed an added burden on all taxpayers. Yet these crimes are rarely punished severely.

Among all the countries in the world, America ranks 20th in life expectancy even though she spends more on health care than any other nation. (See Figure 1.9) Nevertheless, the death rate, particularly for blacks, is near that of Third World nations.

Over the past ten years AIDS has particularly threatened the black community. Of the 200,000 AIDS deaths, one quarter were black.[15] Moreover, black children make up 50% of children with AIDS.

So how we are living - our lifestyle - is actually killing us. Wake up America! You are on the decline.

America's schools have fallen behind almost every industrialized country. Almost 30% of today's youth drop out of school.[16] About 90% of those who stay graduate incompetent in reading, comprehension, and math and science scores, contributing to a society of 10%-20% functional illiteracy.[17] It's difficult to walk the school grounds or even the school building's hallways, without being robbed or threatened by someone with a gun or a knife.

With all of these problems, it's clear that America is in serious trouble, and is on her deathbed. With all of these problems you would think that the leadership would be coming up with creative solutions for the people. But instead of facing the truth and focusing on fixing the problems, the leadership engages in what's called "grid-lock" politics. The leadership either cannot come to terms over the source of the problems or maintains a state of denial of the problems, while scapegoating the poor.

If a person comes with a realistic solution, they are called "radical." I ask you, if your vital signs physically looked like America's, would you want business as usual? Would you want moderation? Or would you want to see some scurrying around as you see in the emergency room of a hospital when there's a life-threatening situation? It takes radical solutions when you're at death's door. America cannot afford a long, protracted treatment for her ills given her desperate condition. These problems need to be diagnosed and fixed **right away**!

# CHAPTER
# 2

# HIDING
# THE LIGHT

Unfortunately, the truth of the real condition of America is kept hidden from the people until conditions become so intolerable that the most uninformed of the people readily sees that something is wrong. Then, scapegoating becomes a necessary tool used by wickedly wise policy-makers and business leadership to re-direct and focus attention away from their own misdeeds and onto someone who is defenseless in the society.

A scapegoat is a person, group or thing upon whom the blame for the mistakes or crimes of others is thrust. According to the Bible, in the book of Leviticus, the word scapegoat comes from the use of a goat, over whose head the high priest of the ancient Jews confessed the sins of the people on the Day of Atonement, after which the goat was allowed to escape. (Leviticus 16:8, 10, 26, 30)

The Honorable Elijah Muhammad taught us that when the door to the raw materials of Asia, Africa and Latin America closes to imperialistic design, the standard of living in America will decline. Those doors are now closing, and the American people are beginning to suffer as a result.

Asia, Africa and Latin America have been the playground for America's economic and leisure purposes. Now that America's ability to extract raw materials from these countries and compete against their products in the global economy has declined, America's standard of living is on the decline. No relief is in sight for America's annual trade deficit of over $100 billion. Labor and other operational costs here make American products more expensive to sell abroad and in many cases even more expensive to sell right at home.

As a result, America buys more from foreign countries, particularly Japan and eastern Europe, than she sells to foreign countries. The door to the world is closing and America is not competing well in the global economy. Thus the American standard of living is going down.

Black people are being positioned by the wickedly wise as the cause of the country's ruin. The scapegoating of the poor sets the climate in America against the American labor class, against the underprivileged, and against black people. There is now a pervasive anti-black attitude. The media feeds this plan of scapegoating black people by portraying us as useless and criminal.

Instead of looking honestly at the problem and coming up with solutions that would give America a future, the leadership lies to the American people and scape-goats the poor and the defenseless for the misdeeds of the American government.

If the American people truly knew their condition and trusted their leadership, they would be willing to take the proper medicine - no matter how bad it would taste - if that medicine would correct the condition. The political leadership has lied about the condition of the country. Some have said that the economy is on the upswing, while we are living in a decline.

If a doctor said you were fine while you were severe-ly ill, and that doctor would not prescribe the proper medicine for your illness, that doctor could be charged and maybe found guilty of malpractice. Well, what about politicians and their unwillingness to prescribe real solutions to the country's problems?

How did America in the past 12 years go from a leading creditor nation to the leading debtor nation? Where was the money borrowed from and to whom is the money owed?

The American taxpayer is now a slave to servicing a skyrocketing debt; a debt that is so large that it sen-tences future generations to the same servitude to this debt because the politicians are not courageous enough to deal honestly with this problem and present the American people with a real solution.

It's dangerous to enslave a people and be the perpet-ual source of opposition to truth, which is the means for freeing the people from ignorance, yet say you believe in God. God has always come to the aid of the oppressed and the enslaved fighting against the rich and the powerful when they deprive others of the basic essentials of life, which are freedom, justice and equality that which is said to constitute the base of this country.

When the slaves were enamored with the riches of Pharaoh, Moses was not able to get his people to listen until he prayed for God's hand to be set against the wealth of Egypt. (Holy Qur'an, Sura 10, Section 9) The more Egypt declined, the more the slaves were inclined to listen to Moses and get up and go for self.

God has always chosen from among the despised and rejected. Whenever there has been a master and a slave, God has always put the solution in the head of slaves. But if America has no respect for human life, or for those who are its former slaves, then America will miss the solution to its problems.

In the Book of Esther in the Bible, there is a prince, Haman, who had prepared a plot to destroy the Jewish people in what was known at that time as the land of Persia. Haman harbored animosity toward the Jews because they did not look upon him with reverence. As a result of his animosity, Haman began to spread rumors about the Jews and misrepresented them as lawless and disrespectful of the king. He proposed to the king that the Jews were worthy of death, "...all Jews, both young and old, little children and women, in one day...and to take the spoil of them for a prey," because of their so-called disrespect for the king's law. (Esther 3:13)

The King, Ahasuerus, who had exalted Haman above all other princes, was therefore receptive to Haman's unjust plot to destroy the Jews. A decree was issued and all Jews were sentenced to death.

However, Queen Esther uncovered the plot. Risking her own life, she approached the king to petition on behalf of the Jews. In this instance, the king was not a sexist. Though the voice on behalf of the Jews was a woman, he listened to her petition, weighed the evidence and determined to spare the Jews. Because the king heeded Queen Esther's warning, he ceased the plot that would have caused unjust death to be visited upon the Jewish people, thereby sparing himself and his country from the wrath of God. If he had been inclined toward sexism, he would have rejected her warning, and he would have sentenced himself and his people to the chastisement of God.

Sexism is sinking the country. Classism is sinking the country. Racism is sinking the country. White supremacy is sinking the country. Black inferiority and a slave mentality are sinking the country.

We must be open to truth, no matter from whom it is spoken, because the ultimate source of all truth is Allah (God). The Honorable Elijah Muhammad taught about those of us who are used to eating from a gold bowl, that if truth doesn't come to you in a gold bowl but rather in an old pot, and you refuse it because it's not in your customary vessel, then your arrogance and foolishness will deprive you of the light that can free you of your condition, and you will ultimately be led to your destruction by your own arrogance.

God has chosen from among the former slaves, the blacks. He has put in the head of the Honorable Elijah Muhammad and in the heads of us who follow him, a light; a torchlight that shows the way out of America's worsening conditions, for blacks and for all of America. But America's treatment of us and America's treatment of the Honorable Elijah Muhammad is like the treatment of Daniel by the proud kings of Babylon. It's terrible that some of those with power and influence label me a Hitler, a racist or a hater, so that they can justify their own people, or agents among our people, in attempts to defame and otherwise harm me. This is hiding the light. This is scapegoating.

The reason leaders desire to hide the truth is to keep the people blind and powerless so that the rich can engage unhindered in feeding their own greed. They don't desire to live in a free society, a just society, and an equal society for all of the country's people. They are rebels against God. As Jesus said, *"Ye are of your father the devil, and the lusts of your father ye will do. He was a murderer in the beginning, and abode not in the truth..."* (John 8:44)

Any man who will not speak or abide in the truth is a murderer of the human spirit and the law of liberty, for only truth gives us true liberty. This is why it is written that *"...it is easier for a camel to go through the eye of a needle, than for a rich man to enter into the kingdom of God."* (Matthew 19:24) The rich are unwilling to really sacrifice to lift the poor because of their basic greed and immorality. Therefore, the rich today are in trouble. Speaking of the rich, in the book of James (5:1-6) it reads: *"Go to now, ye rich men, weep and howl for your miseries that shall come upon you. Your riches are corrupted, and your garments are moth-eaten. Your gold and silver is cankered; and the rust of them shall be a witness against you, and shall eat your flesh as it were fire. Ye have heaped treasure together for the last days. Behold, the hire of the labourers who have reaped down your fields, which is of you kept back by fraud, crieth: and the cries of them which have reaped are entered into the ears of the Lord of sabaoth.*

*Ye have lived in pleasure on the earth, and been wanton; ye have nourished your hearts, as in a day of slaughter. Ye have condemned and killed the just; and he doth not resist you."*

As it was in the days of Jesus, so it is today. The rich have been found wanton and wanting, and God's judgment is upon them in America.

# CHAPTER

# 3

# GREED AND LEADERSHIP'S STATE OF MIND

The fundamental motivation in this society is greed and the preying upon the weak of the country and the weak of the world, versus sharing wealth in cooperation with the weak and the poor. Greed is defined as a selfish desire for possessions and wealth beyond reason. When greed is exercised in the society, it is reflected by division among the people.

The whole society is modeled after division and that old mindset of haves and have-nots; of the lord and the servant; the slavemaster and the slave; and the male and the female. These mindsets are reflected in the doctrines of white supremacy and black inferiority, and are perpetuated by the root problems of greed and pervasive immorality.

Speaking on the period after slavery, one of our giants, W.E.B. DuBois, tried to warn the South to move away from greed as the foundation of the society's economy. In *The Souls of Black Folk,* W.E.B. DuBois wrote:

*"Atlanta must not lead the South to dream of material prosperity as the touchstone of all success; already the fatal might of this idea is beginning to spread...For every social ill the panacea of Wealth has been urged, - wealth to overthrow the remains of the slave feudalism; wealth to raise the "cracker"; wealth to employ the black serfs, and the prospect of wealth to keep them working; wealth as the end and aim of politics, and as the legal tender for law and order; and, finally, instead of Truth, Beauty, and Goodness, wealth as the ideal of the Public School."*[18]

Rather than dealing head on with the root problem of greed, it appears that throwing money at problems is the thing that America has done most, and done most foolishly. There are many things money cannot solve. The response to the riots during the '60s in Los Angeles, Watts and Detroit was to throw money at the problem. But this did not get to the root problem of continued injustice to black people. The same problems among urban black people persist today. In fact, the problems have worsened.

America also throws away the taxpayer's money by commissioning valuable studies yet the government never really uses the results for the purpose of doing good. Though many of these studies are unpopular, they provide solutions that America could perhaps use to stop the ship of state from sinking. But this mindset of greed has permeated every aspect of society, blinding the rulership to the results of studies that they themselves have commissioned. Greed was in the very genesis of this country. Greed was at the root of the founding of this country. Greed was at the root of slavery, and it persists as a central problem to this date.

The business community is so filled with greed that the bottom line means more to corporate America than the lives of the people and America's well-being as a nation.

Now both the business community and the nation are in trouble, and the business community is asking the taxpayer (through the government) to bail it out.

Rather than accepting less profits, businesses close plants, export jobs overseas and negotiate deals with the government that take America further into debt.

The military budget is as great as during war time, yet senators in states with strong weapons industries fight for military budget increases so that contracts can remain in their states - in effect saying to hell with the country and its budget woes.

Allah (God) has a way of showing His disapproval to those who are wise enough to read the signs. FEMA, the Federal Emergency Management Act, was enacted to finance emergencies and recoveries from national disasters. Natural disasters are God's way of indicating His displeasure and are a sign of impending doom. FEMA doesn't have enough money to pay for the earthquakes that hit San Francisco during the World Series a few years ago. FEMA does not have enough money to pay for Hurricane Hugo, Cyclone Omar, the hurricanes in Hawaii, the tornadoes that have torn up Tampa Bay, and Hurricane Andrew. All of these catastrophes increase the budget deficit. And more of these catastrophes are on the way to America with ever-increasing

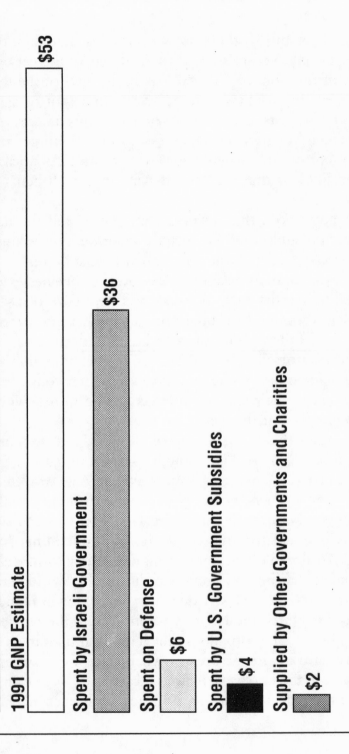

# Figure 3.1: U.S. Taxpayers' Subsidization of Israel *

1991 GNP Estimate — $53

Spent by Israeli Government — $36

Spent on Defense — $6

Spent by U.S. Government Subsidies — $4

Supplied by Other Governments and Charities — $2

Source: Central Bureau of Statistics, Statistical Abstract of Israel 1991; Israel State Budget, 1991

★ In billions of U.S. dollars

rapidity. This is God's way of nudging or forcing government leadership to accept real solutions to the country's problems. Jehovah used ten plagues against Pharaoh. Those ten plagues, including natural calamity from snow, rain, hail and earthquakes, are seen in the world today, particularly in America.

There is a certain arrogance and false pride among the leadership that encourages the wrath of God. The leadership would like to keep up a reputation in the world that is not supported by its people. America gives away billions to other countries while she is suffering at home. What is the basis for this spending? It's the lust for power and the maintenance of imperialism.

America gives $4 billion in aid to Israel, whose population is just 6 million, while giving just $1 billion in aid to all of sub-Saharan Africa, which has more than 600 million inhabitants. This shows us clearly where the government's priorities rest. (See Figure 3.1)

America wants to keep up a posture and uphold white supremacy in the world while she deprives her people at home. America spent $10 billion for the homeless Jews in Russia while millions of her own people are living under bridges and in cardboard boxes or on the streets. These are yesterday's workers - and America's former taxpayers and soldiers - but America turns a deaf ear to their suffering to maintain her image abroad as a superpower. In the Bible it is asked, *"...what shall it profit a man, if he shall gain the whole world, and lose his own soul?"* (Mark 8:36) There is a principle that charity begins at home. What good is it to spread democracy abroad and lose it at home? Has America lost all of its senses and become blinded by greed, arrogance and foolish pride?

Greed represents a moral problem. It's a spiritual disease. The country needs a spiritual awakening and a spiritual change that will lead to moral consciousness. Even some of the spiritual teachers must be freed from this spiritual disease.

Qualified spiritual teachers have to be urged to teach the populace, particularly the rich, against their greed and immorality and put the people in a position to make sacrifices. Without the will to make sacrifices the country will go down. The rich have to be imbued with that spiritual and moral desire to sacrifice more of their profits to help America survive. Or else, the future, which is already mortgaged, will most assuredly be lost to revolution and anarchy.

Look at the situations in Somalia and Liberia, where bad government was replaced by no government. The Qur'an teaches us that when you see things happening at a distance, you should take heed because the same thing could be making its way toward you. Don't think that America is safe from revolution and anarchy. If government and business leaders continue to hide the truth - which is the basis of the will to sacrifice - then the country is doomed.

Politics, in the negative sense, is the game of gaining power at the expense of truth. It's the distrust of government, coupled with the need for more disposable income, that causes the people to desire a tax cut. Quite often, politicians lie so that they can ride into the seat of power on a false promise. Then when they get in the seat of power they scapegoat the poor. They take money from the taxpayer, and from the elderly who have paid their dues to the society, to cover the federal debt, thus spending the country's future.

The state of mind of the entire society has been corrupted. The state of mind of the leadership is that which has sentenced the followers and the nation to death.

Human beings are like fish. Fish swim together in schools. Like fish, the people follow the leadership. If the leadership goes in the wrong direction, so go the people. This is why it is written that the people are like sheep, easy to lead in the wrong direction and difficult to lead in the right direction. This is why the people are in need of the Jesus, who is called the good shepherd by virtue of his will and capacity to lead in accord with obedience to Divine law and principle.

According to the Competitive Policy Council, a group commissioned by the government to study America's economic plight, the country has no long-term vision and its incentives are perverse.[19] All the planning and incentives in the society are oriented toward the short term, meaning that there is no long-term vision.

In the Bible, it reads that *"Where there is no vision the people perish..."* (Proverbs 29:18) Having no vision means that you are spiritually blind. The leaders are blinded by their own greed and inordinate self-interest, and they have blinded the people by hiding the truth. In the Bible the question is asked,*"...can the blind lead the blind? Shall they not both fall into the ditch?"* (Luke 6:39) The Honorable Elijah Muhammad said that the "ditch" represents hell. The country is descending into the abyss of hell.

What contributes to the inability of the leaders to plan the future of the nation, as other industrialized nations are doing? By trying to maintain a posture of slavemaster and slave; of ruler and ruled; of have and have-not, with black people and even with poor and working class whites, America has clouded the light and lost its vision.

**This is why, in our judgment, solving the problem of black people is central to solving the problems of America. America suffers from a crisis of mind, based in denial and never really coming to terms with the moral questions of greed and inordinate self-interest, which is exemplified in its treatment of black people.**

A crisis exists among leadership that has no vision and is bent on trying to overlord itself over the masses. A crisis persists among people whose professed values of liberty, justice and equality, and the basic essentials of human rights, are corrupted by greed and inordinate self interests, so much so that they are blinded to their own sickness.

## THE POOR HAVE NO VOICE

It's sad that most of the congressmen, the representatives of the American people, are from the wealthy class. The wealthy and the privileged in this society, who have benefitted most from the federal debt, corporate restructurings and plant relocations, are the people charged with representing the poor. Can they adequately represent the poor?

In the 1992 presidential debates a young woman asked the candidates how can they, who have never known suffering in their lives, lead the American people and bring a healing to what ails the country? The closest people to the proper representation of the masses and their suffering are the blacks, women, Native Americans, poor whites and Hispanics. In the

Congress, the closest representative of the poor is the Congressional Black Caucus. Each year, they have developed and presented before Congress a budget that would keep America strong while at the same time looking out for the masses of America's people. Each year, their efforts have been belittled and their budget has been voted down.

It's our peculiar relationship with suffering that has prepared us for leadership today, and it is precisely because we have an intimate understanding of the devastating effects of being subject to greedy, racist, sexist, immoral leadership, that we have a chance, if reformed, to be a torchlight for ourselves and for all of America.

In truth, the poor are voiceless in society as it is presently structured. Every president in recent history has been of the privileged class. This does not mean that being wealthy disqualifies one for leadership Being wealthy does mean that there is a lack of an experiential vantage point that we must pay careful attention to.

It was Mr. Ross Perot, among all the candidates in the '92 presidential election, who recognized - and openly stated - that the wealth he has achieved is from the poor. Now he sees that same country and those same working-class people who gave him the opportunity to be a billionaire, going down the tubes.

Jesus said in his sermon on the mount, *"Blessed are the poor in spirit: for theirs is the kingdom of heaven."* (Matthew 5:3) How can you be blessed and poor at the same time? How can you be blessed when you're barely surviving or can't feed yourself? Jesus meant that out of the poor will come the Jesus who can lift the poor. This is why the rulership of that day feared Jesus. In him they saw the end of their power and the end of their rule.

The man, Jesus, was sent because no one was speaking concerning the real issues of the poor. Jesus became the advocate of the poor and got in trouble with the rich. The poor today need a Jesus. The poor today need an advocate who will stand for them and speak out to the rich on their behalf.

## A SOCIETY OF PERVERSE INCENTIVES

It's the greed for short-term profit that has generated an entire society devoid of values and that alienates the poor and the few non-greedy. Most of the incentives and many of the laws in the society are corrupt.

As an example, more is paid to professional athletes than society's teachers. The teachers have to work two jobs to make ends meet, yet they are responsible for shaping the future by shaping the minds of our children. I'm happy to see the brothers and sisters in sports and entertainment making money. However, I am appealing to them, what are you doing with the money to help your people? What kind of opportunity is paraded before our young, when there are only about a thousand positions for our talented sports figures but there are millions of black children suffering, who can never become professional athletes to escape from their condition?

Legislative policy and tax law is perverted to work for the rich. The political action committees (PACs), the lobbyists, the special-interest groups, all work for the rich. The rich get a capital gains tax break. The corporations get to write off special deductions and interest on loans. The poor get nothing but the burden and the blame. The lowest rung of the workforce is made idle through plant closings and America spends next to nothing to retrain them to make them useful in the economy.

Pride and arrogance are part of the leaders' mentality. This spiritual disease is what blinds them to the true formula for success because they're trying to keep up a posture in the world that is out of step with the will of God and the demands of the time. They want to maintain themselves as the great imperialist power, the overlord, the slavemaster, the god beside God.

It doesn't profit America's leaders to lose the respect of the people who have sacrificed to build this country. The American worker has worked and sacrificed to build this country. The corporations, the high-paying government jobs, the fine material possessions, all of this was built on the backs of slaves and the labor class. It is wrong for companies to leave the poor and the working classes in the lurch - conceding manufacturing to other nations under the guise that America is becoming a more service-oriented economy.

It's the failure to deal effectively with this old mentality of slavemaster and slave that has taken the country to the brink of ruin. If America does not deal with this mentality - which is rooted in the outdated relationship between black and white - then America is doomed.

Manufacturing is the bedrock of self-independence. Why should America let others produce for her what she can produce for herself? Why should Italy produce all the shoes while the American shoemakers sit idle at home? Why should your garments be fabricated in Taiwan while your own plants close and collect dust? America could see the simple solutions to its problems if America were not blinded by greed and that old mentality of slavemaster and slave. Both mentalities have to be broken and replaced with a sense of community, humanity and fairness structured on truth and the principles of justice and equality.

## THE MENTALITY OF BLACK LEADERSHIP

Black organizations and leadership must focus on self help. We should create a forum in which we can convene regularly to discuss the troubles of our people and develop solutions that we can execute on our own.

Each black organization and every black leader has a role in the upliftment of our people. We must recognize and respect each other's role and learn to work with those with whom we may be at variance ideologically. We should consider establishing a united front for the purpose of converging our efforts to meet common objectives over one, three, five and ten years.

As a people, we must recognize and understand that in order for America to survive she must tighten her belt, and all of her citizens will need to make sacrifices. The country is not in a position to give away because it has mortgaged its future. Even its Veterans, who have fought to maintain America as the number one military power, will need to make yet another sacrifice.

Therefore, black leadership cannot go to the government to beg it to provide a future for us. Putting the beg on America is not a wise program for our leaders to advance on behalf of the people. That old slave mentality that keeps us at odds with one another and dependent on white people has to be broken.

Black leadership must champion the strategy of turning within to do for self. Meaning, we must teach our people to use our talent, time and money, and pool our resources educationally and financially, to address our troubles. Whatever America decides to do, our actions cannot be dependent on the actions of a benevolent, white, former slave-master.

Even though this country owes us reparations, in her present condition what she owes will stay on the back burner or not on the stove at all. We must work harder to address our own problems. We must also provide the country with solutions that benefit us as well as the whole, to pull the country to a state of strength. Perhaps, when the country's condition improves, we can speak more effectively about what is owed to us for our services, past and present, to repair our condition.

## AMERICA ON THE BRINK OF ANARCHY

Without an advocate for the poor, without a new state of mind in America, the country lies on the brink of anarchy. Anarchy is the complete absence of government. It's a condition of political disorder, violence and lawlessness in the society. We saw signs of it in Los Angeles after the Rodney King verdict.

Anarchy may await America due to the daily injustices suffered by the people. There really can be no peace without justice. There can be no justice without truth. And there can be no truth, unless someone rises up to tell you the truth.

The Nation of Islam can be of assistance. We desire to reason with the political and economic leadership, with the hope of formulating a cooperative effort for the benefit of us all. We want a new relationship in which we can work together for the good of the whole.

However, the desire of the wicked is to harm me and to destroy the idea that I carry so that black people and all who would listen cannot and will not make the type of progress that time demands. This is no different from the desire of the wicked to destroy Martin Luther King, Jr., Malcolm X, Elijah Muhammad, Marcus Garvey, Frederick Douglas, Sojourner Truth, Harriet Tubman, Denmark Vesey, and all who have stood on behalf of the poor and rejected.

It appears that there is a genocidal plan against black people. The desire of many of those in power is the maintenance of white supremacy. Whites and their institutions have created inferior-minded black people with a slave mentality. There are those who do not wish to see us as equals in the society. So generation after generation of black people have been corrupted with a slave mentality, and generation after generation of white people have been poisoned with the doctrine of white supremacy.

However, the presence of truth condemns both mind-sets. The time of white supremacy and black inferiority is over. This is why it appears that an organized effort is underway to destroy black youth. Youth are more readily inhaling the ideas and truths that can free the mind from the former controlling forces of white supremacy and black inferiority. Their hearts and minds are inclining toward interest in self-knowledge. As a result, there are those who fear that our youth are no longer afraid to resist white supremacy and reject its efforts.

Notice how the police and the judicial system do not treat our youth as children. Our 14-year-olds and 18-year-olds are killed in police stations, and the police offer lies to explain their deaths, such as they hanged themselves with their own shoestrings and other such foolishness. All too often, the Justice Department of the U.S. government is weak in pursuing the truth about what the black community believes are wrongful deaths at the hands of law enforcement. They fear our youth. They fear the gangs because prior to the gangs the police were the only gang in town. Often the police are running or compromising with the dope business, the prostitution business and the criminal element in the society. Many officials do not desire to see young blacks organized, fearing that they may join together and one day do unto law enforcement what the law enforcement officers have been doing unto us.

This is not to say that all police are corrupt. But when we see so many incidences of police corruption, such as the Rodney King case and others, then the entire law enforcement system loses our trust.

The youth have the basic qualities of what it takes for seeking liberation. The leader has to have helpers to fulfill the vision. The helpers cannot be afraid of the enemy. God rides in on our faith in Him. This is why when Moses was leading the people into the Promised Land, the older people were left to wander in the wilderness until they died out, and their children were taken into the Promised Land. This was done because their children did not have the fear of Pharaoh or the love for Egypt's wealth, nor did they have the fear of the giants that inhabited the land that Allah (God) had promised them.

If we don't make earnest moves toward real solutions, then each day we move one day closer to revolution and anarchy in this country. This is the sad and yet potentially joyous state of America. She stands at the doorway of disaster and yet at the threshold of unlimited progress. It all depends on who is going to guide the country and what kind of guidance he or she will give. The time does not demand a hypocritical approach to solving the problems.

The time demands sincere commitment to principles of truth and justice. Those of us who were harmed by what went on in the past, and still persists today, are capable of forgiveness. America will be surprised at how quickly the human spirit forgives when amendment, atonement and repentance are set on the plate.

# 4

# FIXING THE PUBLIC SCHOOL SYSTEM

By all measures - literacy, the dropout rate, test scores, plans to attend college and the cultivation of truth and principles among today's youth - the school system has failed. It's hard to understand how my generation, born in the thirties and forties, was at least able to read and write, yet America has made so many advances in the society since then, but today's generation is less able to read and write than mine.

As mentioned earlier, it is estimated that from 10% to 20% of Americans are functionally illiterate. The public schools can't keep our youth in the classrooms long enough to make them literate. The high school dropout rate has reached 30%, and of those who return, only 80% of 19 to 20-year-olds gain their high school diploma.

Today's students cannot point out, on a map, the countries that are in the news shaping the course of world affairs. Many of today's youth cannot read well enough to perform the basic functions of entry-level jobs. This is a pluralistic society yet the people have no knowledge of each other or even of themselves, except for the folklore promoted by and about white people - such as Columbus sailed the ocean blue in the year 1492 and "discovered" America, and that George Washington never told a lie.

Education is vital to each individual's life chances and the quality of the society as a whole. There's a direct relationship between having a high school diploma and one's ability to get a job and to secure one's future financially. A young adult between the ages of 25 and 34 is more than two to five times more likely to be unemployed if he or she does not have a high school diploma.[20] This means that if young adults do not at least gain a high school diploma, his or her chances for surviving in the society are severely crippled.

If America does not wake up and recognize the consequences of perpetuating the current system of education, then the country's fate is sealed. If America is unwilling to destroy the old system of education in order to create a new system of education, then America's status as a world power will quickly fade away in a generation or so.

Solving the problems in the public schools is not so much an issue of adequate funding as it is an issue of establishing the right priorities and following the successful models right in our midst as evidenced by the record of some private schools, Catholic schools,

schools in wealthy communities and others - including the Muhammad University of Islam.

## THE PURPOSE OF EDUCATION

Let's deal with what education is supposed to be as opposed to what it is in America. One of the things that separates man from beast is knowledge. Knowledge feeds the development of the human being so that the person can grow and evolve into Divine and become one with the Creator. It's not one's maleness or femaleness, being black or being white, rather it is our growth and reflection of knowledge that distinguishes us from the lower forms of life.

Education is supposed to be the proper cultivation of the gifts and talents of the individual through the acquisition of knowledge. Knowledge satisfies our natural thirst for gaining that which will make us one with our Maker. So true education cultivates the person - mind, body and spirit - by bringing us closer to fulfilling our purpose for being, which is to reflect Allah (God).

The second purpose for education, after self-cultivation, is to teach us how to give proper service to self, family, community, nation and then to the world.

The problem in today's education is that the root motivation is the acquisition of wealth and material things rather than cultivation of the human spirit. In a study conducted by Dr. Harold Stevenson, professor of psychology at the University of Michigan (in which he compared American schools to those in East Asia) the educational deficiencies of America's youth were traced to the motivational forces promoted by America's culture. In response to a "wish" question, Chicago children tended to wish for money and material objects while Beijing children wished for educational goals. Dr.

Stevenson concluded that "clearly, a challenge in the U.S. is to create a greater cultural emphasis on education and academic success. But we must also make changes in the training of teachers and in their teaching schedules, so that they, too, will be able to incorporate sound teaching practices into their daily routines."

## PUT GOD FIRST

True and proper education starts with the knowledge of God. And yet God is taken out of the schools. It is ridiculous that the school day does not begin with prayer. God is the author of all knowledge, so why should He be taken out of the schools?

Recognition of God is the proper beginning point for understanding every discipline. If we cannot honor God, the Supreme Teacher, then how can the children honor their teachers? We have this thing all backwards. You don't pledge your allegiance to a flag, which is merely the symbol of a nation. You pledge allegiance to God, and you work for your flag and country.

A while ago I coined the phrase, "he who gives the diameter of your knowledge prescribes the circumference of your activity." If you gain a limited knowledge then you restrict the possibilities of what you can and will achieve. The capacity of man's brain is infinite. Therefore, the greater one's knowledge grows, the greater becomes one's sphere of activity until it encompasses and reflects mastery of self and mastery of the universe.

The knowledge of God is infinite. I would argue that leaving God out of our schools limits our education and confines the scope of what we are equipped to do and achieve.

As an example, in the recent movie on Malcolm X we saw a young man who looks like many young men today, except that he rose from a low life of crime and ignorance into the man who a great many now admire. Malcolm rose to his heights because he was taught the knowledge of God, self and others by the Honorable Elijah Muhammad. Because Malcolm was taught outside of the sphere of white supremacist teaching, he never lost a debate, even against the most learned of the society and even though he had just an eighth-grade education. God was present and foremost in Malcolm's "true" education, and this is why he achieved what for others would be an impossibility.

## TEACH THE TRUE KNOWLEDGE OF SELF AND OTHERS

Every human being requires a knowledge of self as part of the proper cultivation of the divinity that is in them. Additionally, and if we hope to live together in peace with others in the society, we must know something of the cultures that make up this so-called melting pot.

A new public school system should relate the curriculum to the self. When we see the curriculum as an outgrowth of self, then we can identify with the curriculum, giving us an incentive to learn. In the Muhammad University of Islam school system, our students' learning is facilitated because they identify with the subjects. They are taught that they are the subject. They are taught, "I am chemistry." Not, "I am a student of chemistry," rather, "I am biology. I am economics. I am history. I am mathematics." When we relate the forces within self to the forces that lie outside the self, this connects us to subjects we are studying in a manner that we can ultimately master those subjects.

Our bodies are controlled by the mind. So mastering economics should not be as difficult with this thought in mind. This body takes in and separates what is useful, puts it to productive use, and eliminates what is wasteful. Therefore, this body is economics and since I am the master of this body, I can master economics.

It's imperative to teach people about themselves, their history, their bodies and their nature so that they can become self masters. Mastery of self is the key to mastery of all disciplines because in some way every discipline is present within ourselves.

Once we have a mastery of self-knowledge, it's important to be taught the true history of the other people who make up this country. This promotes mutual respect for the members of the human family, lending to a peaceful and productive society.

This is why black history should be studied, not only by black people but by white people. As we have developed a respect for white people by knowing their history and great accomplishments, whites will develop a respect for black, Native American and Hispanic people and all the peoples of the Earth when they know the histories and contributions of others to the onward march of civilization in a pluralistic society such as they claim this is.

It is absolutely a vital necessity that the people who make up America should be a part of the study of those who call themselves Americans, and in that way we grow to respect one another. Even if we never grow to love one another, mutual respect is all that is really required to make the nation truly great.

If America believes in pluralism, a new system of education must be developed that gives all human beings their proper due. The current study of American history is nothing more than the indoctrination of Americans in the ideas of white supremacy and black inferiority. At best, blacks, Hispanics and Native Americans learn how to use wit and skill to maneuver in a hostile environment, but they are not taught how to create new circumstances that make freedom, justice and equality, life, liberty and the pursuit of happiness realities instead of just words on a piece of paper.

The fundamental philosophies of Western civilization are rooted in white supremacy. You can't bring a black child into that kind of educational environment and produce a child who loves and respects itself. You produce a child who bows down to white people and looks at white people as being God. I'm not saying it's wrong to respect another human being, but it is totally inappropriate to worship another human being - who is no better than yourself - as though they are a god beside Allah (God).

If whites patterned themselves after God then we could follow them. But they have done quite the contrary. And so we can't follow their example and permit our children to be destroyed with false knowledge that breeds in white children a superior attitude and breeds a sense of inferiority in black children and an attitude that says we can not accomplish what we will.

This is why Malcolm X left school and went into criminal life. There seems to be a practice of identifying young, brilliant black children, particularly black boys, and casting in their minds suggestions that stagnate their development and kill their upward movement. Evil suggestions were made to Malcolm, to me (and others in the past) as students in the school system. I know that these same evil suggestions are being made to tens of thousands of today's young black children.

One of America's greatest crimes was and is depriving us totally of the knowledge of self. This is a crime of immeasurable dimension. Having been deprived of the richness of our history deprives us of the springs and motives of human action that would tell us the possibilities that are within us. If you know what your forebears did, then you know the realm of possibility for you. If you are deprived of that history, then you have nothing to connect yourself to as a person. You are left vulnerable to attach yourself to the circumstances you are given, and in a white society everything that is given to us has a Eurocentric perspective that has historically been hostile to black people.

We as black people never, therefore, get a root in ourselves, but focus instead on white people - their vision and accomplishments - as the standard by which we judge our possibilities. Further, we are subtly and overtly taught that we can never measure up to them and achieve their level of accomplishments because, by nature, we are inferior beings.

## HONOR THE PROFESSION OF TEACHING

Teachers are the stewards of the proper cultivation of the people. Without teachers, we have an underdeveloped people. With an underdeveloped people, we set the stage for a backward society, which we are witnessing in the present-day reversal of America as a world power.

The Honorable Elijah Muhammad said that education is the torchlight of civilization. If the educational system is declining, this is a sign that the whole of the civilization will follow into a state of decline.

What are we going to do about a country that can give a man millions of dollars to throw a ball into a hoop and will not pay an educator an adequate salary? What does this say about our understanding of education and its importance? We have a serious misplacement of values and priorities that needs to be corrected.

Teachers must be compensated commensurate with their role in society. We have to restore honor among those who choose and are employed in this noble profession. Better compensation of education professionals at the public school level can help us attract and retain those whose talent is otherwise channelled into corporate America and other endeavors that pay more and provide lifestyles that are treated with respect and honor. In so doing, the school system can be more selective and use only those teachers who have a genuine love for people and a desire to bring the best out of our children. Surely with all of the recent layoffs in corporate America there must be an abundance of qualified people who can provide our children with better education.

## FOCUS ON RAISING STANDARDS, PARTICULARLY IN MATH AND THE SCIENCES

Only about 16% of America's high school students graduate competent in math, according to the National Assessment Governing Board. The figure is just 2% for

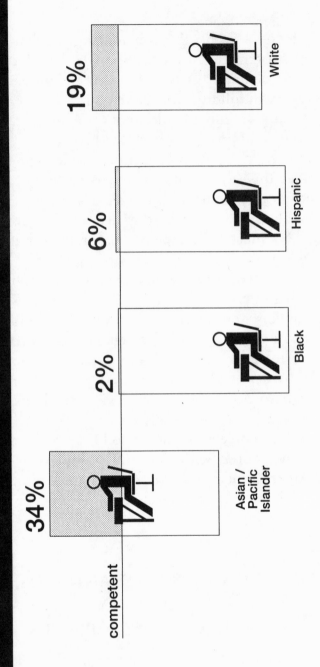

**Figure 4.1: U.S. High School Student Math Competency**
Percent of 12th graders who are competent in mathematics

competent

34%
Asian /
Pacific
Islander

2%
Black

6%
Hispanic

19%
White

Source: National Assessment Governing Board, 1991

blacks and 19% for whites. (See Figure 4.1) So everyone is suffering. The problem is even deeper when we reflect on how other countries are performing relative to America. Youth in Japan, the Netherlands, Hungary, England, France, Scotland, Finland, New Zealand and Hong Kong are performing significantly higher than the American high school students in math scores. (See Figure 4.2)

This country needs to set a standard of being No. 1 in math and the sciences and focus its curriculum to achieving such. America should also set a dropout rate objective of 0% versus the 30% level that she is experiencing right now.

Improving the math scores, the dropout rates and college enrollment of America's youth is not an impossibility. Just look at what the Nation of Islam has achieved with our students, and working with a barebones budget. Four of the first high school graduates from Muhammad University of Islam were featured in the 1992 fall edition of Who's Who Among American High School Students. Four of our first high school graduating class of 10 students scored in the upper five percent of all high school students in the United States on the California Achievement Test. All of our first graduating class are either in college now or are on their way.

## HOLD CLASSES YEAR-ROUND

One of the reasons the Muhammad University is so successful is that we hold classes year-round. There is an old saying that an idle mind is the devil's workshop. There are no jobs for today's youth. If they are not in school, and the parents are not at home watching them,

## Figure 4.2: International Mathematics Achievement Comparisons

Performance of 13-year- olds from fourteen countries in relation to U.S. 1980 to 1982

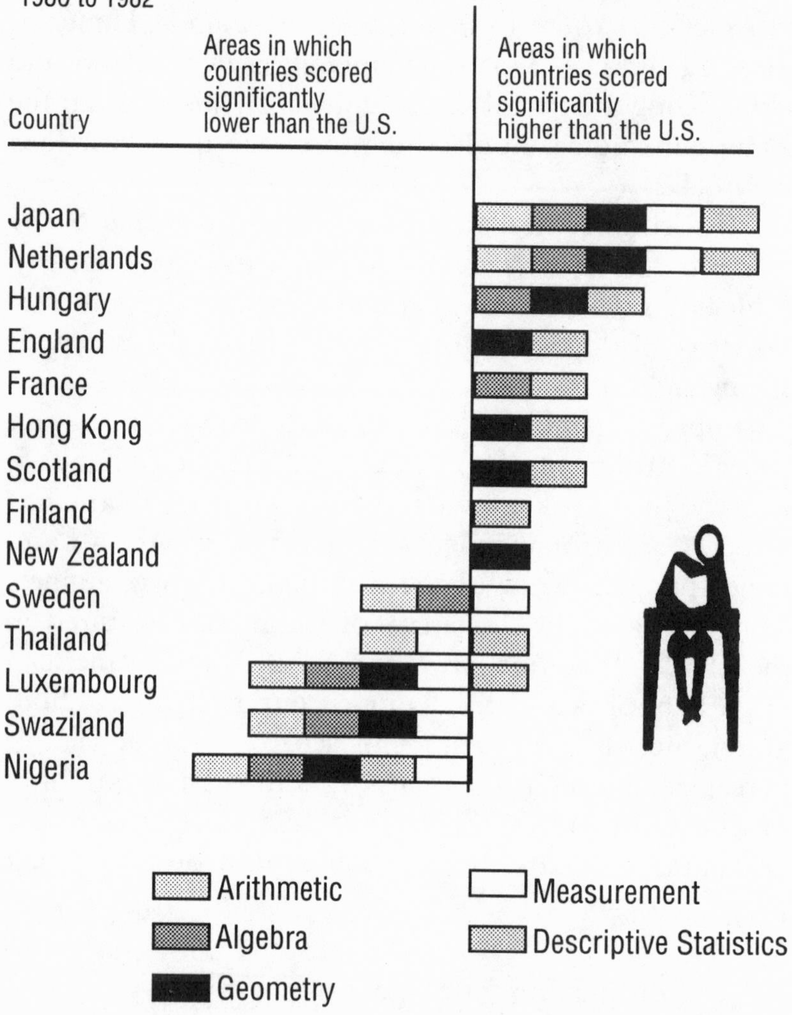

| Country | Areas in which countries scored significantly lower than the U.S. | Areas in which countries scored significantly higher than the U.S. |
|---|---|---|
| Japan | | |
| Netherlands | | |
| Hungary | | |
| England | | |
| France | | |
| Hong Kong | | |
| Scotland | | |
| Finland | | |
| New Zealand | | |
| Sweden | | |
| Thailand | | |
| Luxembourg | | |
| Swaziland | | |
| Nigeria | | |

Arithmetic    Measurement

Algebra    Descriptive Statistics

Geometry

Source: International Association for the Evaluation of Educational Achievement, 1989. National Center for Evaluation Statistics, 1991.

and they are not working, then what are they free to do? Idleness and mischief.

America must take notice and reflect a deeper understanding of contemporary circumstances in educating today's youth. The current school-year calendar is built around the agricultural societies of the 1800s, and not the post-industrial urban society of today. This must change.

## SEPARATE SCHOOLS FOR BOYS AND GIRLS

We must understand that the natures of men and women are different, and that therefore we need separate schools for boys and girls through high school. In my view, it's intellectual cowardice not to recognize and act wisely concerning the differences between the sexes.

We have had great success with separate schools for the sexes at Muhammad University of Islam. Many leading private schools have achieved their prominence by having separate schools. We can all see that the female is not like the male. But it's deeper than that. Because of the difference between the sexes, if we hope to truly develop the person, the school has to train him according to the nature that God gave him and train her according to the nature that God gave her.

There is something to be said for freeing young minds from unnecessary distractions so that they can be cultivated and mature into the knowledge of self so that they may relate to others on a mature and respectful level. The problem in encouraging separate schools for the sexes is that some believe separation would lead to inequality, and this is a valid concern.

Therefore we must ensure that girls are equally exposed to every bit of knowledge that is available. For too long, society has deprived women of certain knowledge and has reduced them, in many instances, to being tools for pleasure. Even the churches, mosques and synagogues have deprived women of certain knowledge and the highest positions of responsibility.

Contrary to popular belief, one of the men who demonstrated the greatest devotion to the elevation of women - through making sure our women have complete knowledge - is the Honorable Elijah Muhammad. It was the Honorable Elijah Muhammad who envisioned women flying planes, navigating ships and serving as ambassadors. He wanted to see women in every field of endeavor, except fields that degrade them. In fact, the avenue to building respect between the sexes is that men be made to respect women for their brains instead of seeing them only as objects for sexual gratification.

Women are the most important element in the nation and the world, because it is through them that new life is brought forth into the world. The woman is not only the cornerstone of family, but when you teach a woman you teach a nation. You can't deprive women of higher learning and produce a great nation.

It is interesting to note that homemaking has all but been eliminated from the school curriculum. The Honorable Elijah Muhammad recognized the importance of homemaking in producing a great nation, and the primary role of women in home-making.

In the Nation of Islam, instruction in basic homemaking skills is an essential part of the curriculum for girls and women. Instead of surrendering garment making to some designer who will give you back a little piece of fabric - and for an extraordinary price - that barely covers our sisters' thighs, our girls and women are taught how to sew and make their own clothing. Instead of surrendering dietary care to the food merchants, Betty Crocker, Sara Lee and Oscar Mayer, our young girls and women are taught how to cook and plan meals for the proper dietary care of themselves and their families.

Caring for the female and giving her a sanctuary where she is free from being preyed upon, to rear her in the best manner, and to protect that sanctuary is the duty of a civilized society. There are sanctuaries for birds. There are seasons when you can't hunt certain animals. But it's open season on women all the time. Women are constantly bombarded by sexual advances and negative messages so much so that they are often put into vulnerable positions that bring evil consequences.

Until society recognizes the value of women, the society will not be properly educated and civilized. One of the ways to embark society on the path of respecting women is to begin with separate schools, through high school.

## HAVE A DRESS CODE

A sanctuary for the proper cultivation of our minds is facilitated by having a dress code. Due to the rampant materialism and sexism in the society at large, youth today, in their mental and emotional immaturity, are vulnerable to the distractions in part caused by fashion and clothing. It's not that fashion and make-up and clothing of themselves are bad, but their primacy as factors in young people's lives must be put in check if we hope to give youth proper schooling.

Having a dress code is a way to minimize class differences and focus the child's attention on learning. A dress code also promotes uniformity and can be a help in teaching young men to be brothers and young women to be sisters. Black women, you have to be known today as one of the righteous, so that when you walk in this maniacal society you will be free from harm's way. A dress code is a protection for you in that you gain the peace of mind from knowing that others have to conform to a code as well as yourself. This lessens each girl's need to feel she has to compete on the basis of promoting her body as an object.

## ESTABLISH DISCIPLINE VIA A PARENT-TEACHER PARTNERSHIP

Parents must be called upon to do their part in preparing their children so that the teachers can do their job. Discipline begins in the home and is vital to the education process. Teachers should be charged with the responsibility of developing a partnership with parents to ensure that each child develops self-discipline. While parents cannot be excused from ultimate responsibility for their children, it is clear that someone has to take the lead. Teachers, who are present in the classrooms with the youth on a daily basis, are sometimes best positioned to take that lead.

## CREATE SCHOOL SAFETY

Nearly half of all high schoolers are victimized by theft or injury each year. Creating jobs in the cities, gun-control legislation and a dope-free America will go a long way in making the schools safe.

Still, we need to do more to curb and guide the natural aggressive tendencies among young men. In the wealthy communities the rich are able to channel the aggression of their young men into meaningful activities. Their youth have better athletic facilities, they go to summer camps, and there are many leagues and team sports in which the young boys can participate. The government, locally and nationally, should place some focus on providing team activities and athletic facilities in channelling the energy and aggression of our young men. This would minimize the need of some of our young males to engage in gang activity to exercise their manhood. This would help reduce the hostility that seeps into the school environment and disrupts the educational process.

There is a system in place to keep a plantation running, for the benefit of the rich and powerful. The only way to destroy it is with proper education, both for the black and white child. Jesus said, *"...except ye be converted, and become as little children, ye shall not enter into the kingdom of heaven. Whosoever therefore shall humble himself as this little child, the same is greatest in the kingdom of heaven."* (Matthew 18:3-4)

The kingdom is not floating in the sky. Jesus taught that the kingdom is within us. However, we can't bring it out unless the heart undergoes a change. The heart must be made humble to receive the knowledge that will heal us of this sick, racist, sexist and materialistic condition that we are in.

We have a knowledge that will free everyone of white supremacy and miseducation so that everyone, black, Hispanic, white, Asian and Native American can join the human family on equal terms. Thus, the Nation of Islam would like to offer its model as a possible way to begin fixing the public school system and to develop a superior education.

The Muhammad Universities of Islam were born from the need to revive, reform and redeem black people who had suffered from the miseducation and hostility toward blacks in the public school system. The Honorable Elijah Muhammad founded the Universities of Islam because he had to reverse the poison that is inherent in the educational system.

Whites too suffer from being deprived of the knowledge that African civilization is the basis of European civilization. Why should this be such a hard truth to tell? Jesus said, *"Behold the fowls of the air: for they sow not, neither do they reap, nor gather into barns; yet your heavenly Father feedeth them. Are ye not much better than they? Which of you by taking thought can add one cubit unto his stature?"* (Matthew 6:26-27)

Do you know that white people have done a great thing for the people of the earth? White people have taught a sleeping humanity the reality of God. Sleeping humanity looks at the moon and writes a song about it. A wide-awake man employs higher mathematics to visit the moon. Everytime a space shuttle takes off you're witnessing the product of higher mathematics and science. No one can mock this accomplishment. Some of us might desire to perform a raindance to make it rain. White scientists will go out and seed the clouds to produce some rain, showing us that the realm of possibility for human beings is only limited by our knowledge and grasp of mathematics and science.

You can accomplish what you will. Man and woman is God, the force and power to make things happen on earth. In the book of Psalm it reads, *"ye are all gods, children of the Most High."* (Psalm 82:6)

This whole universe is rooted in mathematics. Therefore, mathematics must become the focal point in a new educational system.

When blacks gained the right to attend non-segregated schools to learn mathematics and sciences, whites began running away fast. Some city colleges were turned into vocational schools to teach us to be carpenters and electricians and data processors instead of scientists, engineers and doctors. Can you imagine that? We're back on the plantation. The Honorable Elijah Muhammad said that without mastering mathematics, the sciences and all branches of engineering, we will never be the builders of civilization.

Mr. Muhammad saw the inherent weakness in the public school system and determined that - for black people to gain the tools needed to build a new reality for themselves - we needed to establish an independent school system, with a new and better foundation. We would like to share our example with the whole public school system. We are concerned that if we don't help the public schools then what will happen to our children who come out of private school but still have to go out into the larger environment? If our children can't change the environment, then the environment will ultimately change our children. So it is not wise to glory in the fruit of our private school. We have to affect the totality of education. However, if we cannot impact the public school system, then it is incumbent upon us as black people to start our own private schools.

The country should look at the Honorable Elijah Muhammad's educational system and use us as a model, instead of condemning us and putting obstacles in our way. God is making a torchlight for America. Let us share with you what He has given us to move us all along the way to a brighter future.

# CHAPTER
# 5

# REBUILDING THE ECONOMY

We are living in the most critical period in American history. We have just witnessed a magnificent event, the changing of power in the White House, from the Reagan-Bush era to President Clinton. I don't know of any other country where the changing of power is done as it is in the United States, with Mr. Bush exiting and Mr. Clinton taking office and each greeting the other in a civilized manner. Though they may not have agreed with each other, they bowed to each other with respect. One party went out and another party came in and America never stopped moving for a fraction of a second.

Although we as black people have suffered at the hands of whites in this country, this is a system of government that we should all study and can all benefit from. It's the greatest system this world has yet produced. Even so, it's in great trouble.

Mr. Clinton has inherited a mess. The backbone of America is bent, her shoulders are overburdened, and virtually every vital organ she has is in need of repair. Mr. Clinton's biggest charge will be to rebuild America's economy. He's young, he's highly intelligent and he's adventurous...and he's in trouble.

President Clinton's inauguration represents a rekindling of hope among those whose hopes have been extinguished over the 12 years of the Reagan-Bush administration. I wonder, what would happen if the hopes of the people were dashed again, after just yesterday coming out from 12 years of hopelessness and dissatisfaction? Can President Clinton save America? This is the challenge that lies before him.

As with Sodom and Gomorrah, Babylon, ancient Egypt and ancient Rome, all of the evils that destroyed those nations and societies are present in America and growing at an alarming rate. If Almighty God did not spare those societies, and in the scriptures it is written, *"For I am the Lord, I change not,"* (Malachi 3:6) then will He spare America? America is compelled to make a change and put itself in a condition where God may be merciful unto her. This would require that President Clinton, the government and the American people recognize the magnitude of the problem and map out a solution that is equal to the enormity of the problem.

President Clinton's charge to rebuild the economy is his biggest charge. He will be successful to the extent that he is honest with the American people, forthright in executing his responsibilities and open to *new* solutions to the country's economic woes.

# REDUCING THE FEDERAL DEBT AND BUDGET DEFICIT

Present and future generations of the American people are held in servitude to financial instruments as a result of the enormous federal debt and the annual budget deficits. The $4 trillion federal debt translates into $16,000 per capita, nearly the entire gross national product of the country, meaning, all of America's productivity goes for naught. The only way to climb out of this kind of hole is to decrease some of the spending and to increase taxes, not only for the wealthy but across the board.

## *Galvanize the People to Make a Sacrifice*

President Clinton must galvanize America to make a great sacrifice to relieve the country of an untenable state of indebtedness. However, in a USA Today/CNN poll conducted in late March of 1993, only 2% of those polled felt that taxes were too low. The American people would not mind being taxed if they could trust that higher taxes would make America strong and relieve her of her debt and provide a brighter future for the children. The American people would not mind being taxed if they had true advocates and representatives in government whom they could trust. So to galvanize the people for making a sacrifice, President Clinton must go before the people and tell the truth, and develop and present solutions that can solve the federal debt and budget deficit problems. President Clinton must galvanize the people to tell their representatives and senators that we don't want "grid-lock" politics. The American people want the elected officials to work together and

# Figure 5.1: 1992 Federal Budget
## (in billions of dollars)

|  | 1992 Budget |
|---|---|
| *OUTLAYS* | |
| Discretionary: | |
| Domestic | 216.2 |
| Defense: | |
| Department of Defense | 300.4 |
| Other Defense | 12.5 |
| Total Defense | 312.9 |
| International | 20.1 |
| Total Discretionary | 549.2 |
| Mandatory: | |
| Deposit insurance | 80.1 |
| Federal retirement | 78.3 |
| Means-tested entitlements | 74.8 |
| Medicaid | 72.5 |
| Medicare | 116.0 |
| Social Security | 284.3 |
| Unemployment insurance | 32.0 |
| Other | -10.9 |
| Subtotal Mandatory | 727.2 |
| Net Interest | 198.8 |
| Total Outlays | 1,475.1 |
| *REVENUES* | 1,075.7 |
| *DEFICIT* | -399.4 |

Source: U.S. Dept. of Treasury (Economic Report of the President 1992, Table 2-3)

solve this country's problems. **Partisan politics must die if America is to live.**

Most politicians are afraid to tell the full extent of the truth that America has seriously mortgaged her future and that to reduce the deficit will require a great sacrifice. This is why Mr. Ross Perot seemed radical during the '92 presidential election, because he spoke very frankly about the problem and what it will take to reduce the debt and deficit.

President Clinton must be careful not to say on the one hand that he desires real change and on the other hand propose moderate moves. Since this generation is already hurting, shouldn't major moves be made to solve the problem so that the future of our children can be saved?

It's a bitter pill to swallow, that after the government, which the American people elected, ran up a $4 trillion debt and adds nearly a $500 billion budget deficit to the debt each year, you, the taxpayer, have to bail the government out. (See Figure 5.1) However, this is the only way for a brighter future to be passed on to the children.

## *Raise Taxes Fairly Across The Board*

Clearly, the government has to raise taxes dramatically to reduce the debt and budget deficit. But taxes must be distributed fairly. The government can't let the corporations and the rich use their lobbyists to continue to lay the burden of taxes on the poor, the middle and working classes.

Did you know that more than 80% of the taxes are paid by the public, while corporations pay about 9% of total taxes, or $98 billion?[21] Corporations have paid a dwindling share of U.S. taxes since their lobbyists have

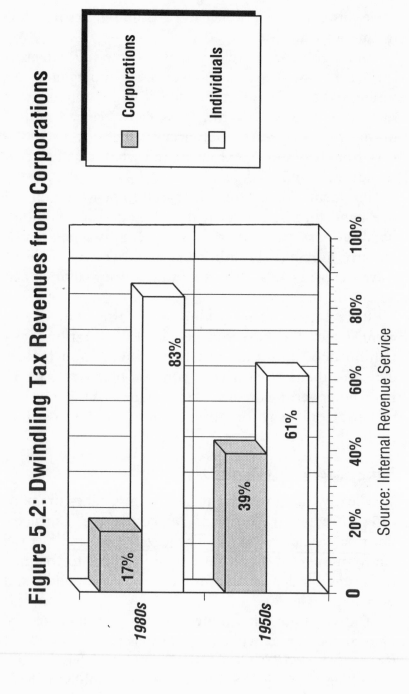

Figure 5.2: Dwindling Tax Revenues from Corporations

Source: Internal Revenue Service

strengthened their power in Washington, D.C. In the '50s corporations accounted for 39% of total taxes. Over the '80s, under the Reagan and Bush administrations, corporations accounted for just 17% of total taxes. (See Figure 5.2) At the current rate, corporations will soon account for a negligible amount of taxes and the public will assume the full tax burden.

Again, there's no effective advocate for the poor in the government. Some of the legislators have become prostitutes for the corporations and the rich. Special-interest groups and lobbyists help push legislation that helps the rich and the corporations avoid and evade taxes. In spite of the minimum tax act, the rich are currently paying half the amount of taxes that they paid prior to the Tax Reform Act of 1986, due to loopholes in the tax code.[22]

Corporations escaped paying $92.2 billion in taxes over the '80s thanks to interest deductions. (See Figure 5.3) Again, this is an example of how the tax code favors the corporations. Corporations are allowed to deduct the interest from money they borrow from the banks. Corporations borrow from the same banks in which the middle and working class people deposit their money. Then, they use that loan to finance the automation of plants and the relocation of their plants to another country. The result is unemployment for the same people whose money was borrowed by the corporations to buy the new technology and to relocate the plant. It's the government, through the tax code, that opened the door for the corporations to exploit the people.

It would be different if the rich and the corporations used their tax breaks to do good by the American people. The American people could look more favorably

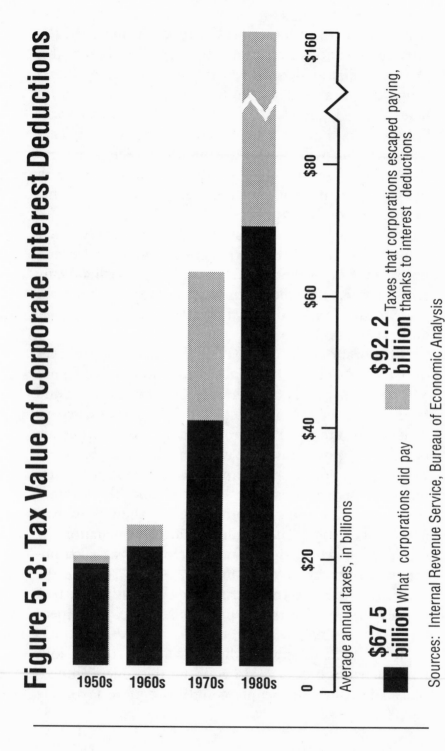

# Figure 5.3: Tax Value of Corporate Interest Deductions

1950s 1960s 1970s 1980s

$20 $40 $60 $80 $160

Average annual taxes, in billions

**$67.5 billion** What corporations did pay

**$92.2 billion** Taxes that corporations escaped paying, thanks to interest deductions

Sources: Internal Revenue Service, Bureau of Economic Analysis

on the wealthy in this country if they used their wealth and the favorable tax law to create jobs, build low-income housing, invest in environmental research, retrain the workforce and develop educational programming that promotes a better lifestyle via the television, but we have seen none of this because the fundamental driving force of the wealthy is greed and not service to the society.

President Clinton will have to summon great courage in his attempt to harness the support of the American people to cut federal spending, raise taxes across the board and extract fairer taxes from the rich and from corporations. This is a very general guideline for the president.

I am no politician, and I am not privileged to the government's accounting books, but there are a few ideas for improving tax revenue that were circulated during the '92 presidential election that seem worthy of attention. Certainly those foreign-owned companies that operate in this country should pay taxes. If they are operating here and extracting money out of this country that the American people need, then certainly they should pay taxes just as other corporations do. Those corporations that get tax breaks to relocate their plants to other countries are another source of tax revenue. If anything, the tax code should be written to penalize businesses that relocate jobs out of this country.

Government revenue can also be raised by enacting sin and luxury tax legislation. The leading cause of so-called accidental deaths in this country is motor vehicle deaths due to drunk driving. Apparently, the legal system has not been successful at curbing drunk driving because drunk driving is still rampant. Why not attempt to gain some justice out of the injustice others suffer due to alcohol use, by levying a substantial sin tax on beer, wine and liquor?  Also, another known killer is cigarette smoking.  The death toll from smoking is in the hundreds of thousands annually, and the health-care bill is in the billions.  The cigarette and tobacco industry does the country no good, and retail purchases should be taxed to do the country some good in the way of debt and deficit reduction.  Use of the sin taxes should be earmarked specifically to debt reduction, and publicly accounted for to the American people.

In terms of luxury items, there are many benefits gained by the rich at the expense of the taxpayer.  For example, the average home costs about $100,000.  However, the homes of the wealthy soar far above this level, and the rich are able to deduct from their tax bill the interest from their mortgage payment.  Why not cap the interest deduction on mortgages over a fair amount, say at a $325,000 mortgage level, and use the taxes avoided by this deduction to offset the debt?

### Enact Debt and Deficit Reduction Legislation

It would seem that "no taxation without representation" has been replaced with "he who controls the tax code determines who pays the taxes," and ultimately, who wins and who loses in the economy.  To restore government accountability, the people must be more empowered with respect to how their tax dollars are used.

President Clinton can help empower the people and restore the people's trust in government by enacting legislation to reduce the debt and deficit.  A law should be passed and enforced requiring the government to eliminate the federal debt in a reasonable amount of time. Another law should be passed that prohibits the government from spending more than it collects in tax revenue. This law would eliminate the annual budget deficits that compound the already enormous federal debt. And last, the people should be given control over a significant portion of their tax payments, say 15%, and have the choice to earmark use of those dollars specifically for debt reduction.

## CUT MILITARY SPENDING

The peace dividend has to be made a reality. At the same time, other countries have to be made to bear more of the burden of the world's security.

The government currently spends in excess of $300 billion on defense expenditures, which is one-fifth of annual government spending. Russia is no longer the military threat it once was, but where is the peace dividend? We have millions who are unemployed, and the infrastructure of the country is decaying. Why shouldn't America use a third or more of its defense expenditures to reduce the budget deficit and generate jobs?

I know the defense industry employs people. But the real job generator in this country is small business, not large business with heavily automated plants. Over the past decade jobs in large corporations, including defense contractors, have been cut in half. Those in the defense industry can be retrained and these highly skilled individuals can be redeployed where they are most needed, such as teaching positions in the public schools (if teaching salaries are made commensurate with the level of the individual's skill).

# Figure 5.4: International Job Retraining Expenditures

| Country | Participation (% of labor force) | Average Duration (in months) | Total Expenditures (% of GDP) | Expenditures per Participant (in U. S. dollars) |
|---|---|---|---|---|
| Canada | 1.1 | 6.0 | .22 | $7,000 |
| France | 2.3 | 2.5 | .28 | $4,600 |
| Germany | 1.5 | 8.0 | .25 | $7,200 |
| United Kingdom | 1.4 | N/A | .22 | $5,000 |
| United States | 1.0 | 3.5 | .05 | $1,800 |

Source: Organization for Economic Cooperation and Development, *Labor Market Policy for the 1990s*, Paris, 1990. Data from 1988.

Countries like Japan and Germany should be encouraged to pay their fair share of world defense. Japan and Germany each pay just about $33 billion toward defense.[23] Why should the United States shoulder the burden of world defense? America simply cannot afford it. Why should other countries like Japan and Germany become world powers while the United States citizens pay their way?

## ESTABLISH A RIGHT-TO-WORK POLICY

There has been a lot of talk about family values. Family values are promoted by the right to work. How can you have 10 million Americans unemployed, and more on the way, and talk about family values? How can you have the unemployment among blacks at twice the level as that of whites for the past three decades and say you want a pluralistic society, with peace on the streets? What family values are being promoted in the black community at the current level of unemployment? The abandonment of families is in direct proportion to the loss of jobs and the attendant loss of self-esteem by those who cannot provide for and support their families.

We need, first of all, a new state of mind among leadership in government and the business community. A new state of mind that sees the right to work as central to having a free, just and equitable society - as central to promoting family values. The government and private business should work together to ensure that every American has a job.

The American people should patronize those businesses that support the right to work, and reject the products of those businesses that want to continue business as usual. The American people should consider boycotting products from those manufacturers that put the American worker out of work, to show the displeasure with the abandonment of the American people.

## FOCUS ON RETRAINING PROGRAMS

The United States spends less than any industrialized country on retraining, less than 5 one-hundredths of one percent of its GNP. (See Figure 5.4) Yet many in the American workforce are under-skilled or skilled in areas where there are no jobs. America has to look after its own just as other countries look after their own, and job training in America is a vital component of looking after the citizenry.

Look at how unjust the government of America was with the soldiers who returned home from Desert Storm, many of whom suffered with wounds and diseases, and cannot find jobs. The soldiers need retraining so that they can be useful in the civilian economy and enabled to feed their families. These soldiers returned home from the battlefront to a cold reception of unemployment and impending poverty. This was their reward for being willing to fight for "freedom and the American way."

President Clinton is advocating a cut of approximately 150,000 United States soldiers currently stationed in Europe, due to the decreased military threat of the Soviet Union. These soldiers are trained in killing. In order to be integrated into the "American way," they will have to be retrained in the skills that are employable in the civilian economy. How will these soldiers respond if there are no jobs upon their return to this country and they are not retrained for civilian employment? Many of these soldiers are black. How will they respond in the streets of America, without job opportunities and without retraining to qualify them for civilian employment? This situation could become a powder keg in the streets, adding to the problem of Vets who have already been stung and hurt by a government that does not seem to care for those who have been willing to offer their lives in whatever theater of war the government decides is right and proper.

## PARTNER BUSINESS WITH THE URBAN POOR AND WORKING CLASSES

When businesses and whites abandoned the cities the tax base was reduced to the point where the cities could not supply an adequate level of services. The infrastructure began to crumble and an increased measure of poverty set in. Whites flood the city at 9 a.m. then flee to the suburbs at 5 p.m. Blacks, Hispanics and poor whites are left behind without jobs, and the result has been that homelessness, hopelessness, gangs, drugs and violence are now taking over the cities.

Here again, we can be of service. Certainly a business would not want to come to a city where crime is rampant. However, wherever there is a substantial presence or influence by members of the Nation of Islam, a relatively crime-free community develops. A peaceful atmosphere has to be returned to the cities in order for business to feel secure in returning. We can help establish that peaceful atmosphere in the cities.

Businesses need to return to the cities in partnership with the urban population. Instead of ceding manufacturing to other countries, why not cede manufacturing to the cities of America, using those most effective at producing a respect for law and order to strive for returning peace to the cities? There needs to be a partnership between business, government (federal and municipal), law-enforcement and the so-called gangs, since the gangs have recently demonstrated their willingness to maintain a truce. Those who have been so destructive, with a change in direction and an earnest commitment by society, can become a most constructive force in securing and rebuilding the cities.

Why not let urban America rebuild itself by using tax incentives to encourage businesses to relocate to the cities? Let the cities become our garment manufacturers, instead of exporting our jobs to Asia and then importing the finished goods back to this country.

The country's trade deficits over the last decade have already surpassed $1 trillion. 80% of U.S. international trade is in the area of manufacturing.[24] So ceding manufacturing back to the cities can help us with jobs and balancing the trade deficit, because, according to the Competitiveness Policy Council, manufacturing generates far higher productivity gains than services. Why should we cede manufacturing and technological advancement to other countries and let America slip further and further behind?

Cede manufacturing to the American people and train the people to produce what is being imported. Cede manufacturing to urban America and give us ownership in that which we produce. We need the government to develop  training programs and a system of rewards and penalties to encourage business to return to the cities in partnership with the people. This is a way to begin to solve the problems in the cities. This is a torchlight for saving America's cities.

# PROMOTE EMPLOYEE OWNERSHIP AND PROFIT-SHARING PROGRAMS

Making black people and urban Americans partners in society will make us more interested in the upkeep and protection of our communities. In the same way that failing companies are offering ownership to their workers, America in general should encourage its people to work, and work better, by making them partners and not just slaves to wages, and low wages at that.

We have attracted tens of thousands of our people to a lifestyle of trying to do something positive for self, and rejecting smoking, drinking, drugs and criminal activity. With the change in lifestyle brought about by following the teachings of the Honorable Elijah Muhammad, we are able to achieve more with less money than others who might earn more but who have a different lifestyle. Manufacturing is often ceded to other countries due to lower labor costs. If the Muslim lifestyle helps us to require less in the way of wages, suppose business would structure a relationship with us where we work for less, but with ownership in the business? If the Nation of Islam were allowed to teach our people, unhindered, then we could effect a change in the lifestyle of our people that would allow us to do more with less wages and salaries.

The challenge to America's business community is to find ways to make the people owners of the businesses and property in their communities, as shareholders and under profit-sharing plans. This is what true economic justice looks like.

Does America have the courage and the vision to restructure its economy for the benefit of the whole of its citizenry? Are government and business genuinely interested in lifting the poor by fully retraining the labor pool and developing a fair partnership that together they may be able to fight competitively in this new age of technology and globalism?

## RETHINK THE OLD
## SLAVEMASTER-SLAVE RELATIONSHIP

The question to black leadership is, can you depend on a benevolent white leader to look after our poor when the country is under such severe constraints? We know that former generations of whites are responsible for putting black people in our current condition. However, conditions force us to think creatively to help ourselves or go down with this ailing economy. By helping ourselves we will relieve the country of some of its burdens, and we will be performing a duty imposed on us by our Creator, which is the duty of doing something to help self.

We must understand that our suffering uniquely prepares us not as slaves, or former slaves, or followers, or second-class citizens, but to be the examples and leaders for humanity. We can help both the former slave and the former slavemaster with what we have been taught by the Honorable Elijah Muhammad and through our peculiar suffering within this racist society. Those of us who have studied and follow the teachings of the Honorable Elijah Muhammad, Marcus Garvey, W.E.B. DuBois and others can be a torchlight for expanding the mentality of the civil rights movement. We stand on our gains today because of the sacrifices of Dr. King, Rosa Parks, Whitney Young, Roy Wilkins and all of those who followed them in the '60s. We respect their gains in the area of civil rights, but we are still not free, which is why we must unite now with a sense of appreciation for those gains and take the civil rights movement to a new level of struggle.

Black leadership must re-orient its thinking to self-help and then come up with creative solutions to our economic plight. We can, we will, we must help ourselves.

## REDIRECT BLACK SPENDING TO BLACK BUSINESS

Black people have $300 billion in spending power, yet, as soon as the dollar enters our community it exits almost immediately. The dollar doesn't circulate to a black bank to pay the mortgage, or to a black-owned grocery store to buy food, or to a black fashion designer or retailer to buy clothing. The money enters our community in the form of a paycheck and exits to a bank, a cleaners, a record store, and to all of those outside the community who provide goods and services for us.

In the *Souls of Black Folks*, W.E.B. DuBois wrote:

> *"The holocaust of war (and slavery), the terrors of the Ku Klux Klan, the lies of carpet-baggers (from the North), the disorganization of industry, and the contradictory advice of friends and foes, left the bewildered slave with no new watchword beyond the old cry for freedom."*[25]

> *"A people thus handicapped ought not to be asked to race with the world, but rather allowed to give all its time and thought to its own social problems."*[26]

It appears that integration has only meant the surrendering of our dollars to others so that they can enhance their lives while our businesses close and our problems remain unattended. We must look like a very foolish people in the eyes of others who nurse themselves to economic strength on our earnings and then abandon us and ridicule us as they advance and leave us further behind. We need to turn constructively inward, pool our resources intellectually and financially, and begin to build a future for ourselves and our children. We must patronize ourselves, as others patronize themselves. This is the way to build a viable economy and earn the respect of self and others.

Black scholars, professionals, organizations and the wealthy among us must be charged with the responsibility of using our resources to build the economic institutions that our people need. We can promote the idea of "buying black," but we must have something manufactured by blacks to buy. More of us need to come out of corporate America, with the skills that we have acquired, and build businesses that service the needs of our community.

## SUPPORT THE NATION OF ISLAM'S 3-YEAR ECONOMIC PROGRAM

We have what we call The 3-Year Economic Savings Program which was designed by the Honorable Elijah Muhammad to raise money for the building up of our economy. By helping ourselves we solve our own problems and lessen the burden on the taxpayers of the country, even though we are taxpayers as well.

The 3-Year Economic Savings Program is not designed to be a burden on anyone. We simply ask participants to contribute a nominal amount to a financial pool each month, for a minimum commitment of three years. In many cases this contribution is made from personal savings that are gained by changing one's lifestyle for the better. For example, smoking is a deadly habit that when stopped can yield a substantial amount of savings. If you are a smoker, how much do you pay for cigarettes? $2.60? Some of you buy two and three packs per day. When you go to a concert how much do you pay? $30? How many meals do you eat and what do you pay for that cheap food? How much do you pay for those drugs in your medicine cabinet, or the ones from the dope pusher?

We don't smoke, drink or use dope. We eat one meal a day and don't excessively go to movies and concerts. So this change in lifestyle results in money in our pockets. The money that we save from cleaning up our lifestyle is money that we can invest in developing economically. Even if America does not help us, with a change in our lifestyle we can begin to use that $300 billion that circulates into our community to build agribusiness, low-income housing, develop clothing manufacturing, establish banks, and create all the economic entities that our people need. If we look at the money we spend each year on frivolous and destructive pursuits, with those who do not have our interests at heart, we can start taking some of this back to ourselves. We can fulfill the scripture, as it is written in the book of Isaiah, that *"...they shall repair the wasted cities, the desolations of many generations,"* (Isaiah 61:4) and create job opportunities and restore dignity to ourselves. We can start rebuilding the cities of Los Angeles and Chicago, where the gangs have been willing to enter into a truce, yet there is no economic plan

# Figure 5.5: Wealth Ownership

| | Black Mean | White Mean | Black% | White % | Black Aggregate* | White Aggregate* | Additional Wealth Needed by Blacks for Parity* |
|---|---|---|---|---|---|---|---|
| Net Worth | $24,168 | $103, 081 | 100.00 | 100.00 | $229,813 | $7,766,444 | $695,808 |
| Interest Earning at Financial Institutions | 3,743 | 20,137 | 43.80 | 75.40 | 15,590 | 1,143,952 | 128,787 |
| Regular Checking | 715 | 1,131 | 32.00 | 56.90 | 2,176 | 48,474 | 3,942 |
| Stock & Mutual Funds | 3,359 | 33,067 | 5.40 | 22.00 | 1,725 | 548,099 | 67,451 |
| Equity in Business | 40,542 | 77,008 | 4.00 | 14.00 | 15,440 | 812,278 | 87,077 |
| Equity in Motor Vehicle | 4,115 | 6,814 | 65.00 | 85.50 | 25,431 | 454,362 | 31,913 |
| Equity in Home | 35,718 | 62,016 | 43.80 | 67.30 | 148,762 | 3,144,555 | 248,111 |
| Equity in Rental Property | 45,542 | 88,155 | 6.60 | 10.10 | 28,582 | 670,827 | 56,083 |
| Other Real Estate | 17,221 | 41,901 | 3.30 | 10.90 | 5,404 | 344,198 | 38,037 |
| U. S. Savings Bond | 657 | 3,133 | 7.40 | 16.10 | 462 | 38,005 | 4,334 |
| IRA or Keogh | 4,109 | 10,802 | 5.10 | 21.40 | 1,992 | 174,168 | 19,989 |

* in millions

Source: U. S. Department of Commerce, Bureau of the Census, *Household Wealth and Asset Ownership: 1984*, Tables 1 and 3.

Note: 1984 data converted to 1989 dollars

to provide these youth with a source of earning a living.

The government should support our efforts with The 3-Year Economic Savings Program because, in reality, we will be relieving the pressure on the government. The government should allow participants to allocate a portion of their taxes, say 15%, to go toward The 3-Year Economic Savings Program so that we can begin to make ourselves self-sufficient.

America will benefit from a productive black people from whom the country might unlearn the mental sickness of white supremacy. It's hard to call me a nigger when I'm productive. It's hard to say we're nothing when you see us as a dignified, civilized people. We are the ones who can destroy the mentality of white supremacy and the thought in others that we are subhuman and inferior by promoting respect among black people by what we accomplish in the way of building and doing for self.

Other black organizations that have proven track records of doing good on behalf of our people should be considered for similar programs. The programs should be initially implemented on a test basis.

## MAKE GOOD ON 40 ACRES AND A MULE

The condition of race relations in America has never been repaired. It has remained a gross wound on the society and has festered over the past hundred years.

Concerning the aftermath of the civil war, W.E.B. DuBois wrote:

*"The Freedmen's Bureau set going a system of free labor, established a beginning of peasant proprietorship, secured the recognition of black freedmen before courts of law, and*

*founded the free common school in the South. On the other hand, it failed to begin the establishment of good-will between ex-masters and freedmen, to guard its work wholly from paternalistic methods which discouraged self-reliance, and to carry out to any considerable extent its implied promises to furnish the freedmen with land....the vision of 'forty acres and a mule', the righteous and reasonable ambition to become a landholder, which the nation had all but categorically promised the freedmen, was destined in most cases to bitter disappointment....the opportunity of binding the Negro peasant willingly to the soil was lost on that day when the Commissioner of the Freedmen's Bureau had to go to South Carolina and tell the weeping freedmen, after their years of toil, that their land was not theirs, that there was a mistake somewhere. If by 1874 the Georgia Negro alone owned three hundred and fifty thousand acres of land, it was by grace of his thrift rather than by bounty of the government."[27]*

Now it is said that by the year 2000 blacks will be absolutely landless.

Today's whites are not the cruel perpetrators of slavery, as were many of their forefathers. However, they are the beneficiaries of slavery in the form of inherited wealth and privilege. (See Figure 5.5) To maintain their position of wealth and influence, many whites utilize the ignorance of black people to manipulate us to serve their economic purposes. Moreover, there is still a group of whites who want to keep blacks in a perpetually subordinate position, or rid the country completely of the black presence.

The legacy of slavery is that wealth has accumulated disproportionately in the hands of today's whites in the form of financial assets and land. There's nearly $10 trillion in wealth in America. However, black people account for only 3% of the wealth in America. The average net worth of a black person in America is $24,000 while for whites it's over $100,000.[28] This is directly due to the legacy of slavery.

If the government is sincerely interested in relieving itself from its responsibility for slavery, then there should be a cooperative effort by business and government to promote the equitable distribution of business, financial assets and land ownership in this country. We never received our forty acres and a mule during the aftermath of the civil war. We remain owed today, to say nothing of the psychological damage for which no amount of compensation can be calculated.

There are millions of acres of federal and municipal land and property currently abandoned or not in use. We can make use of that land by developing agribusiness to feed our own who are hungry, and the hungry of the world, and by building low-income housing for the urban homeless, for the poor and for the working class. This is our spirit. The government should consider selling or leasing us the land and property at a price that is mindful that America owes us reparations for the holocaust of slavery.

Within America black people must develop in the area of agribusiness and show America a better diet. We must acquire fertile territory on which to harvest our produce. If people are to be healthy they have to change their diet. When they change their diet they need access to non-chemicalized, overly processed food. The food companies don't have the incentive to teach right and do right by the American people. We must have land of our own from which we can produce the food and create the circumstances that will improve our condition and serve as an example for the rest of America and the world.

If the U.S. government can repair Japan and Germany after W.W.II and send aid to foreign countries, why can't America bail out its own suffering people? If America won't, we must use what we have been blessed to gain from our sojourn here to help our people ourselves. The alternative is our own destruction.

Look at how we are uprooted and displaced from the cities in which we live. Using the tools of poverty, gangs, drugs and weaponry, there is a plot to move blacks out of the inner cities so that whites can move back in. The cities are devastated to the point that when enough people move out, when enough buildings are vacated or destroyed, the developers move in and create a new reality out of the ghettoes, and reap huge profits in so doing. A new reality sets in with fine homes and condominiums and paved streets and prospering businesses, for white people. This is called urban renewal, or gentrification. You've seen it. It's going on in every major city right now.

Where is the government going to put black people? Wouldn't it show more vision to help us repair ourselves? We need a new relationship with the government that enables us to use our tax dollars to repair ourselves, our communities, our cities. We're not looking for a give-away. We're willing to repair the damage that America's forefathers created, and since we pay taxes in this country - since we have fought and died for this country - black people want the government to respect and represent our interests in that the government should help us to help ourselves. This is what democracy is supposed to be about.

## SAY FAREWELL TO WELFARE

The total cost of AFDC and food stamps is about $40 billion annually, and about half of this $40 billion goes to poor blacks. (See Figure 5.6) This is not a real economic burden on the country in the way that entitlements for the wealthy, the military budget, health-care costs, and tax evasion by the rich and the corporations impact the federal budget. We are the scapegoat and we are positioned as a burden on the taxpayer.

My mother was a welfare recipient, but she never used it as a crutch. When I completed high school, my mother stopped accepting the welfare checks, thanked the government for their assistance and said that she would support her family without the welfare check from that point. So I know that welfare is necessary as a safety net for society's poor, particularly when they suffer economic hardship.

I want to focus on a spiritual condition that we need to fix. The Honorable Elijah Muhammad taught us that it's time for us to say farewell to welfare. Welfare means farewell to self-reliance and self-respect. The nature of man is to be productive. America is going against the nature in which God created the human being when America has masses of people not being productive. About one and one-half million black families live on AFDC and the food stamp program.[29] It's not our fault that we are poor, but it becomes our responsibility to make ourselves productive. This is

## Figure 5.6: Welfare Expenditures

| Race | | How Long on AFDC | |
|---|---|---|---|
| White | 38.8% | Less Than 7 Months | 18.2% |
| Black | 39.9% | 7 to12 Months | 13.2% |
| Hispanic | 15.7% | 1 to 2 Years | 17.3% |
| Asian | 2.4% | 2 to 5 Years | 26.3% |
| Other or Unknown | 3.3% | Over 5 Years | 25.0% |

| Children in Family | | Mothers Age | |
|---|---|---|---|
| One | 43.2% | 21 or Younger | 15.6% |
| Two | 30.6% | 22 to 29 | 39.5% |
| Three | 16.1% | 30 to 39 | 31.5% |
| Four or More | 10.1% | 40 or Older | 13.4% |

| Fathers of the Children | 1988 | 1973 |
|---|---|---|
| Divorced or Separated | 30.3% | 46.5% |
| Deceased | 1.7% | 5.0% |
| Unemployed or Disabled | 8.6% | 14.3% |
| Not Married to Mother | 54.6% | 31.5% |
| Other or Unknown | 4.8% | 2.7% |

Source: Andrew Hacker, **_Two Nations: Black, and White, Separate, Hostile, Unequal,_** p87.

why when our people come into the mosque of the Nation of Islam, we put them to work. We don't believe in non-productive human beings. When a person is not productive they're destructive. So America is producing its own destruction by putting millions of people out of work, and on top of that, diminishing unemployment and welfare benefits.

Instead of scapegoating labor and the poor, the government should be retraining its people so that they can hold a productive post in the society. So retraining must be a component of welfare. I am pleased to see President Clinton moving in this direction with regard to welfare.

Will President Clinton have the courage and the vision to rebuild America's economy? In addressing the country's economic ills, will he do right by the poor and black people? Will the president commit to a major overhaul of the economy, or just window dress the problem so that he can keep the support of the rich and corporations in order to win the next election?

Can white America stand to see an employed, productive, dignified black America? Is white supremacy so embedded that America cannot stand to see blacks trying to qualify themselves to become equal to the best in civilized society?

Know that if America can't stand to see us make this kind of social progess, then, the only solution is complete separation in a land of our own. Know that if we cannot get justice within this country or via separation, then the country is destined to go the way of ancient Egypt, ancient Rome, Babylon, Sodom and

Gomorrah and the way of the British Empire. Unless America is willing to break that mind-set of a slavemaster and deal with this problem of black people in America with justice, then the country will not survive.

# CHAPTER

# 6

# DEVELOPING AMERICA'S MORAL BACKBONE

Duty to God should always come first in everything we do. The more we neglect duty to God, the more the whole of society falls into disrepair. No matter what policies are formulated in Washington, D. C., or what programs are implemented in the schools, if God is not kept first and foremost in our endeavors we will not be successful. The society will continue in its decline toward death and we will remain in need of a deep and widespread healing.

One of the things that has to happen in order to effect a deep and widespread healing is to recognize that we need to be changed at the root. Once we can admit to ourselves that something is wrong, then we are able to seek guidance to correct what is wrong.

Mr. Ross Perot did something during his campaign that taught a lot of lessons. When Mr. Perot bought half hours of TV time to express his analysis and solutions for the problems of America, he competed against TV shows that were very popular, yet his show's ratings outperformed the shows he competed against. What does this indicate? It suggests that the American people hunger for knowledge that will give them solutions rather than foolish entertainment. I believe that the corporations that buy and back the inordinate amount of foolish TV programming have misread the earnest desire of the American people to save themselves and the nation.

## CONVENE SPIRITUAL LEADERSHIP TO SPEARHEAD A MORAL REJUVENATION IN AMERICA VIA THE AIRWAVES

The root of the problem in America is spiritual, necessitating a spiritual solution. President Clinton should call for a convening of the spiritual leadership to spearhead a moral rejuvenation among the American people. Representatives of all races and all faiths should be brought to Washington, D.C., to hold conferences with President Clinton and government leaders toward the aim of developing programs for building the values and moral backbone of America, and for building better race relations.

Without a moral backbone, the nation cannot stand upright. Those creatures that have a backbone but cannot stand upright are known as four-legged beasts. Those creatures that have no backbone at all generally belong to the species called serpents. It is written in Genesis that beasts and serpents caused the fall of man. The destruction of beasts and serpents is foretold in the book of Revelation. As human beings, if we hope to enter the kingdom of heaven, we are meant to aspire toward righteousness, rather than act in a manner that makes us worse than the lowest of animals, the beasts and the serpents.

A convening of the spiritual leadership with the leadership in government is a first step toward building the country's moral backbone. The central problems we should focus on are the basic value of human life, greed, criminal behavior and the treatment of women. It's the mistreatment of women that is the first act of criminal behavior in the society.

Mr. Perot's success via the airwaves suggests that the American people are ready to be taught via good and beneficial TV programming. Why not dispatch the spiritual leaders to develop educational and spiritual programming that will expand knowledge, develop character and thereby lead to a more enlightened and harmonious society across race, class and sex lines?

Broadcasters and other influential members of the media must also be summoned and shown their responsibility in the development of America's moral character. They are one of the main culprits in numbing the people's moral consciousness in a way that allows the people to engage in evil with impunity. If they would participate in a concerted effort to strengthen America's moral backbone through enlightened TV programming, America's chances for success would be greatly improved.

## PROMOTE A CULTURAL REVOLUTION THROUGH THE ARTS

The artistic community has historically been in the vanguard of social change. What is now needed is for the artistic community to lead a cultural revolution. On the physical level, man is what he eats. Spiritually, *"...as he thinketh in his heart, so is he..."* (Proverbs 23:7) If the American people are constantly fed filth and garbage through newspapers, magazines, television, movies, plays and music; if the public, like the proverbial swine, has become a lover of filth; and if thoughts guide behavior, what do the thoughts of the American people produce? Do the thoughts of the American people produce rape, incest, murder, theft, greed, and the destruction of family and the institutions of society? I would argue that the answer is yes.

Therefore, along with summoning the spiritual leadership to convene with leadership in government, the artistic community needs to be shown its responsibilities to the overall mental and spiritual health and well-being of society and the world. Our gifts, as artists, are a blessing from God. We have the responsibility of the proper use of our gifts. Additionally, movie producers, record producers and publishers all have a responsibility to the spiritual, moral and mental well-being of the American people.

Will it profit the major producers and publishers to become filthy rich by feeding filth to the American public at the cost of the survival and progress of the nation? Who among the artists, producers, agents, publishers, writers and directors would like to be, in part, responsible for helping America become as the modern Rome, Babylon, Sodom & Gomorrah, all of which earned the wrath of God? If the artistic community would take up the challenge, and if the business community would not use its money to back filth and foolishness, if the real hunger and thirst of the people for knowledge and quality entertainment were fed, the country could be turned around almost overnight. A positive direction could be charted for the American people, which they must move toward if they hope to be saved from the country's present course.

The Bible refers to the people as sheep, who, as the Honorable Elijah Muhammad said, are easily led in the wrong direction, but hard to lead in the right direction. The people are responding to what the leaders have offered them, which is called "popular culture." The people's appetite has been made insatiable for filth. If the leaders turn away from evil and indecency, then the people will turn. If the artists turn away from filth and indecency, then the people will follow. This is why it is written in the scriptures that the people need a "good" shepherd. In every field of endeavor, good leadership has to be asserted to turn corruption, greed, filth and indecency into righteousness.

## PROMOTING POSITIVE RELATIONSHIPS BETWEEN THE SEXES

### *The Basis of Proper Male/Female Relationships*

Neither male nor female can fulfill their relationships to each other until they are first properly connected to the source of all creation, which is God. This is why the divorce rate is so high, and the dissatisfaction rate in relationships between the sexes is even higher.

The natures of male and female are different, but they are meant to complement each other. In the absence of knowledge, the different natures of male and female can work destructively against the self and against the union of both. The fundamental knowledge that is absent in male/female relationships is the knowledge of how we should relate to God and each other.

It is our disconnection from God that is at the root of failing and improper relationships between man and woman. This is a very deep problem in the relationship between black men and women. One of the major crimes perpetrated against us when we were brought into slavery was that a true and proper relationship between us and God was severed. The slavemaster stood in the place of God and made us relate to him as master in the place of God. To this very moment, no matter how much we say we believe in God, Jesus and Muhammad, many of us subconsciously relate to whites as master, and "God" is just a word that we use.

Every human being has the potential to be a reflection of the Most High, but we also have the potential to be the very opposite. We have taken the lower desires of self, the urges and the lusts, and made them our god in place of the true God. Sometimes we talk about wanting to be right, however, until we earnestly desire to be right, we will never move toward right. We have to earnestly desire righteousness for righteousness' sake, not for the sake of some reward or for fear of some punishment.

Being righteous will give us peace of mind and power. When we act in accord with what is right we can lay down at night with the peace of mind that comes from knowing we haven't done anything or anyone wrong. This is where the true and real power of our minds comes from. The ability to focus on something and summon the power of our being to bring into reality our vision, in this time period, is truly based upon our striving to be right.

After a negative relationship, part of healing has to be that we be removed from the environment that facilitates our doing wrong. Most of us are not strong enough to fight against wrong influences when we remain in a wrong environment. It behooves us to make a change when we face circumstances like this.

It's counter-productive to flirt with trouble. A woman who wishes to stay away from fornication or adultery cannot spend too much time around an old boyfriend. He will only want to use you until he is reformed. He may try to get you in the wrong place, at the wrong time, under the wrong circumstances, so you will do the wrong thing one more time. After you do the wrong thing, you feel dirty. God is trying to make a new mind in us. If we are fortunate enough to hear and accept God's truth, it will take root in us and wrong won't seem right anymore.

In the Holy Qur'an it reads, *"We certainly sent messengers to nations before thee, but the devil made their deeds fair-seeming to them. So he is their patron today, and for them is a painful chastisement."* (Sura 16, Verse 63) We have lost the criteria for judging our own actions because the standard of good has been confused and evil has been made to look "fair-seeming."

The human being has a grand purpose. It is wrong to take a woman or a man just for pleasure. Responsibility goes along with intimacy. Caring and sharing goes along with intimacy. Every time you engage in intimacy without responsibility, without caring, without commitment, without sharing, without honest communication, it lowers your self-esteem, self-respect and your self-worth until you begin to see yourself and others see you as a person without value. This is because every time we submit to our lower desires, we actually are beginning to make *nothing* of ourselves, while Allah (God) wants to make *something* of each of us.

If we cannot be strong alone, then we have to be among those who are strong. If we attach ourselves to strength because we desire to be strong, then we shall become strong. Allah (God) is the source of strength, goodness and purity. So your first connection should be to God, then connect with the strong and keep away from the environment that produced your weakness lest the forces of weakness and death destroy the new life that is trying to bud in you. When we are strong enough, then we can go back to the environment of our weakness with the strength to change it.

You don't need a mate until you find out who you are and what you need and hope to achieve in life. When thoroughbred horses are mated, the breeders carefully examine the stud and the mare with an eye for what they hope to breed from the two. We can learn a lesson from the mating of horses. We should learn that in order to get what we want in a relationship, we have to first understand who we are and how to identify in others that which we need to help us in our development into Divine.

### Toward Eliminating Rape & Molestation

Two million women are reported to be beaten by their spouses each year. Three-quarters of a million women are estimated to be raped each year. The resulting psychological damage is of enormous magnitude because you corrupt a nation when you corrupt a woman, which is why God set up strong laws to protect women and to protect the family.

Rape is the murder of the essence of a female. It's no wonder that many women who have been victimized by rape or incest have difficulty in relating to men and their own families. Women are created to provide heaven, consolation, comfort, peace and quiet of mind to their mate. What she provides she is meant to give freely, but men must earn the right to this gift. When a woman is raped she may never again be able to give of her essence, unless God intervenes to heal her. When the nature is killed, only God, Who created our natures, can revive it again.

After a woman is raped or molested, there is often no such thing to her anymore as a decent man. She could lose all faith in men and become a lesbian, which is very prevalent, or a prostitute or a free-for-all woman who will give herself to any man who asks.

We regard crimes against women as extremely serious. Rape and child molestation are not only crimes against the individual, they are truly crimes against the society and nations. The people must be taught properly and given guidance for conducting themselves among their fellow man. Then, if they refuse to abide by the laws that are designed to protect women and the family, harsh punishment can be given.

In Saudi Arabia we have a society that is relatively free of the pervasive crime and many of the violent crimes that plague America. The strong Islamic law and exemplary punishment of transgression of the law has helped in making Saudi Arabia a country with less crime and savage behavior than any other nation on earth. In my travels to Saudi Arabia I have actually seen open safes, with untold amounts of money, yet no one would dare to attempt a robbery. Merchants can merely cover their merchandise with a cloth while they go to pray, without the fear of being burglarized. This is, in part, because the punishment for such crimes - the threat of losing a limb or your life - is so severe that no one wants to take a chance.

In order to correct savage behavior, knowledge must be imparted to the people and the society's institutions must be corrected. This would give the people a fair chance to become civilized. Then, for those who still transgress the law, harsh penalities including the death penalty can be justifiably used.

However, this society has failed its people. The institutions are failing the people. Therefore, knowledge has to be imparted and the institutions must be corrected before the death penalty can justifiably be established. When you have a society as wicked as this one is becoming, where the behavior of the people is so savage, the strong law Moses applied to Israel must be used to bring the people out of savagery until love of the law could be nurtured. That same strong law of the time of Moses may have to come to America.

For those who have suffered a sexually violent crime such as rape, incest or molestation, healing starts with justice. The problem is that very few women raped in this society get justice. The worth of women has to be restored, at all costs. The woman's worth has to be reestablished. Women must help to reestablish their own value by never giving themselves to any man unless there is love and commitment. And society must do a better job of teaching the people the value of human life, and correct its economic, penal, educational and spiritual institutions.

## *Homosexuality*

None of us is worthy to judge another based on their sin. While homosexuality is not approved by God, and since none of us are without sin, we don't have the right to cast stones against another manifestation of sin. Jesus taught that when we offend in one law, we offend in all. Since we are all sinners, and all of us have fallen short of the glory of God, then we are really unfit to judge one another.

However, we must not allow the standard raised by God, as given to us through the mouth of His prophets to be destroyed, and say, "well, anything goes." To adopt a mindset that whatever you do is alright, as long as it is between "consenting adults," is wrong. It is written in the scripture that no effeminates would see the Kingdom.

We must change homosexual behavior and get rid of the circumstances that bring it about. We must change all behavior that offends the standard of moral behavior set by God through His laws and prophets.

As a civilized society, we should look with compassion on the sinner while abhorring the sin. It is wrong to preach that Jesus is a saviour and redeemer and in the same breath speak so harshly in our judgment of an aspect of sin that we may not be guilty of personally, while we offend the law of God in some other respect. This is why the people have been so hard on the preachers whose actions are far less than the standards that are preached. Many of us preach the standard raised by God as though we have no weakness at all. We must preach the standard for guiding human behavior, but we must do it in a manner that allows the public to see that we too are striving to live up to that standard.

### *Promiscuity & Premarital Sex*

We must respect and honor women if the nation is ever to be great. When we do not have a proper appreciation for women, this is reflected in women's roles in the society. Women should be active in every field of endeavor except those that degrade them. Why is it

# Figure 6.1: Out-of-Wedlock Births 1950-1988

| | Black | White | Multiple |
|---|---|---|---|
| 1950 | 16.8% | 1.7% | 9.9 |
| 1960 | 21.6% | 2.3% | 9.4 |
| 1970 | 37.6% | 5.7% | 6.6 |
| 1980 | 56.4% | 9.3% | 6.1 |
| 1988 | 63.7% | 14.9% | 4.3 |

Source: Andrew Hacker, *Two Nations: Black and White, Separate, Hostile, Unequal*, p.80

that a woman who is exceedingly beautiful must model filth and indecency? Why can't she model something beautiful and righteous instead of being a saleswoman for filth? Why is it that if she is a singer we end up seeing more of her bosom than hearing her voice? The righteous are sick of the degradation of women. The maintenance of women as sex objects is destroying the society.

Two-thirds of black children are born out-of-wedlock and half of today's black youth are raised in a home where only a mother is present. (See Figure 6.1) One-fourth of America's young girls become pregnant by their sixteenth birthday. Clearly, the relations between men and women have become rampantly irresponsible. Women are being used, and allowing themselves to be used, as sex objects. This moral problem, in part, is undermining the cultivation of proper family life.

We breed hostility with the thoughts we carry during promiscuous relationships. We have sex for recreation instead of its divine purpose of procreation. The thought we have in mind is not wanting to have a baby. So now in our communities violence is prevalent. Carjacking is prevalent, and we wonder what the world is coming to.

Think back to when you were producing the children of this world. You didn't tell the woman that you would stand by her if she had a baby because you love her. The minute she told you she was pregnant you didn't want to see her anymore. She then puts the thought of murder in her womb in response to your callous treatment of her and her pregnancy. Then, you leave her abandoned and embittered with a baby, your baby, to take care of. So she brings forth and raises a

# Figure 6.2: Who Gets Child Support

Percent of single-parent families headed by a female that receive support or alimony

| White | Hispanic | Black |
|:-----:|:--------:|:-----:|
| **43%** | **18%** | **17%** |

Source: Center for the Study of Social Policy

child after her own thinking, and we wonder why today's youth are so rebellious.

More than half of female-headed families do not receive child support or alimony. (See Figure 6.2) This problem is most acute among blacks where 83% of our female-headed households do not receive assistance. The irresponsibility in our treatment of each other is reflected in the children that we produce.

When we place a plant in a different pot, often that plant goes into shock. Imagine how children are affected when they are abandoned or consistently moved into different homes or different environments. When the relationship between husband and wife becomes cold, what happens to the children? We produce a hard generation of children by our not understanding or caring about the dynamics of how thoughts are transmitted during sex and during pregnancy. We must learn to act responsibly in the male/female relationship, for the sake of ourselves, our mates, our children and our future.

### *Abortion*

Some of us are pro-life and others are pro-choice. I am both. I'm pro-choice in that women should have the right to choose to whom they will commit their lives. So don't regret bearing life from that one to whom you have made a commitment. I'm not for any woman or man having the luxury of pleasure without responsibility. There is a procreational aspect to sex, and it's the neglect of this aspect that gains us disapproval in the sight of God. No one should be free to kill the fruit of the womb not understanding that what you are producing could be the answer to your own prayers and those of your forebears.

Nearly 15 million babies were aborted in the '80s, according to the Center for Disease Control.[30] The annual rate of abortions is currently 1.5 million per year. For every four babies conceived, three are born and one gets aborted. And this does not account for so-called illegal abortions.

Most women do not realize what they're carrying. We have to bear the responsibility of our actions. This is why no woman should lay down with just anyone. Don't let biological need force you to do something that you will regret later.

My mother tried to abort me three times. Although she eventually decided to have me, the effect of her thinking is on me. However, God has used that effect for His purposes.

When you think to kill during pregnancy, you produce after your thoughts. And we wonder why the children are so rebellious and violent.

Today's youth are much more violent than their counterparts were in the period prior to Roe versus Wade. We must ask, what contributes to this difference?

It now takes two working parents to provide for most households. In most instances, today's working mothers cannot bond properly to their newborns. Instead, the babies bond to a plastic milk bottle, rather than the warmth of mother's bosom. Parents give their children away to day-care centers to warehouse their children during the day while the parents are at work. Today's children are bonded more frequently with teddy bears and plastic bottles - cold, heartless things - but rarely to a human being.

The unwanted financial burden a newborn can bring and the coldness that exists between the parents fills the atmosphere with desires for abortion and neglect of the children. Callousness and the thought of murder permeates the atmosphere, sanctioned by the government through Roe versus Wade, and justified by the economic need for both parents to work, that removes the mother from forming a proper bond with her babies.

As my mother lay dying on her bed, she told me while cradling her womb, "son, I thank God for what He allowed my womb to produce." She prayed that God would forgive her for even trying to kill such a precious child. The womb is a sacred house, a sacred place where you and God, or you and satan, operate to produce what you see walking the street.

Society should not promote abortion. This is equal to the promotion of murder and recreational sex when the recreational aspect of sex should be special and reserved for those who have made the proper commitment.

However, I am not in favor of letting the product of rape or incest come to term. Abortion is justified in these cases, along with those instances where the mother's health is at risk.

The penalties for negligence by the male in fulfilling his obligation to support his children should be better enforced. This measure would help reduce the feeling on the part of some women that they must have legalized abortion in order to protect themselves from negligent men. However, the government has the responsibility to its citizenry of creating jobs so that today's fathers can support their families.

Avoiding non-marital sex relations should also be promoted by parents, teachers, the clergy and members of the artistic community, even though this measure is perceived by some as unrealistic.

# FIGHTING CRIME

### The War on Drugs

Most of the violent crime on the streets is drug-related. In 1992 $12 billion was allocated to fight the war on drugs, according to former President Bush's Budget for Fiscal Year 1993. The bulk of the money was spent on law enforcement and about a third went to treatment and prevention.

According to a 1989 survey by the National Institute on Drug Abuse, blacks only make up 12% of drug users but FBI figures indicate blacks account for 44% of all drug possession arrests. In spite of the fact that whites sell most of the nation's drugs and account for most of its customers, blacks and Latinos continue to fill America's jails.

According to the Wall Street Journal, a survey in California revealed that where 70% of people sent to prison for drug offenses were black, more than 63% of public drug treatment slots went to whites.[31] Again, racism at work.

Ridding Mayfair Mansions in Washington, D. C., of dope traffic and rehabilitating the addicts is a success story of the Nation of Islam, at no cost to the country. We have a Dopebusters program that has been very successful and is applauded by the communities in which the Dopebusters or Nation of Islam security are present. How is it that with nothing we can do what the government has not been able to do with $12 billion?

We are an example for America. If America sincerely wants to rid the society of the scourge of drugs, it should let us help. It only makes sense to follow what works, and fund what works. The Dopebusters program, if properly funded, could help to rid the nation of drug traffic and addiction. We have a proven record. Since America is either unwilling or unable to curb addiction, it should let us rehabilitate our own. We are getting the results. Why shouldn't America back us? The government can help us by patrolling the borders and keeping drugs out of the country. But let us help in handling the streets. It's in America's own self-interest.

### *Recognize and Penalize White-Collar Crime*

All of the street crime that has been committed does not add up, in terms of dollars, to what Milken and Boesky did with their junk-bond scheme.

In a white supremacist world, white-collar crime gets overlooked relative to the focus on blacks and street crime. Why make blacks the focus as the real criminals? W.E.B. DuBois wrote:

> *"Even today the masses of the Negroes see all too clearly the anomalies of their position and the moral crookedness of yours. You may marshal strong indictments against them, but their counter-cries, lacking though they may be in formal logic, have burning truths within them which you may not wholly ignore, O Southern Gentlemen! If you deplore their presence here, they ask, who brought us? When you cry, deliver us from the vision of intermarriage, they answer that legal marriage is infinitely better than systematic concubinage and prostitution (that we experienced during slavery). And if in just fury you accuse their vagabonds of violating women, they also in fury quite as just may reply: the rape which your gentlemen have done against helpless*

*black women in defiance of your own laws is
written on the foreheads of two million mulat-
toes, and written in ineffaceable blood. And
finally, when you fasten crime upon this race as
its peculiar trait, they answer that slavery was
the arch-crime, and lynching and lawlessness
its twin abortions; that color and race are not
crimes, and yet it is they (color and race) which
in this land receive most unceasing condemna-
tion, North, East, South, and West."*[32]

I am not excusing street crime. But justice is a two-
edged sword wielded by truth. It cuts both black and
white and has no regard for one's station in life. But in
America there is no justice in the courts and in the penal
system for blacks and the poor. We have nothing more
than a system of laws - laws to protect the interests and
the property of whites.

## *Support the Nation of Islam's Prison Reform Ministry*

The prison system is not set up to reform. It's a
dead end. In a Philadelphia study, it was found that
35% of all males had been arrested at least once.[33]
Fifty-four percent of those arrested at least once were
arrested a second time. Sixty-five percent of those
arrested twice were arrested a third time. And 72% of
those arrested three times were arrested a fourth.

The rate of recidivism, or tendency to return to
criminal habits, indicates that there is no real reform.
In fact, the inmate's propensity toward criminal behavior only worsens after going to prison. And $18,000 of
the taxpayer's money is spent per year per inmate to
keep them in prison.[34] In effect, billions are spent each
year to create and maintain hardened criminals that
remain the outcasts of the society.

When you look at what the Muslims are doing with our prison program, in the midst of you, here again you see a torchlight. Muslims are relatively crime free, and our rate of recidivism is lower than in the main. We respect law and order. Since so many of the inmates are our people, why not let us reform them and help to save some of the taxpayer's money. Why not let us handle the inmates and lessen the taxpayer's burden. We can handle the inmates for less than what America is paying now. And better, we can reform our people and make them productive members of society.

## BEGIN REFORMING BLACK INMATES BY HELPING THEM MAKE A NEW BEGINNING IN A LAND OF THEIR OWN

America has not found a way to curb crime and reform those in her society who consistently break her laws, particularly in the black community. The fact is that due to the high rate of recidivism, most of the street crime in this country is perpetrated by the same set of people. Instead of being reformed, a substantial number of people are recycled through committing crime and then being incarcerated again and again. The threat of street crime to life and property, and the great cost to the American taxpayer for warehousing people in jails and prisons, continues unabated.

We have an idea for addressing the problem of crime and reforming the so-called criminal, that can at the same time relieve some of America's burdens and even elevate her stature in the eyes of God and the nations of the earth.

America, and the nations of the earth, are in competition for developing the resources of Africa - the next significant economic growth opportunity in the global economy. Blacks in America could help to foster the relationship that could cause America to be first in line in trade relations with Africa and the development of her mineral resources - which is the prize sought by every nation that would hope to be a world leader in the 21st century.

However, America's foreign policy and relations with other nations is largely a reflection and the result of her treatment of the different ethnic and racial groups within her borders. If America would improve her treatment of black people, she could leverage that improved treatment to foster favorable relations with Africa. Also, if America would develop an enlightened foreign policy toward Africa, this would lead to stronger trade and economic opportunities.

We are proposing that America - by encouraging development in the black community and by helping us to make a new beginning on the continent of Africa, first with the inmate population - could win a place in the hearts of Africans that would gain for America a strong foothold on that strategically important continent.

If we look at what Europe and America did for the Jews of the world by creating a state for them in what was called Palestine, we ask: Why can't this model be used again to create a state for those black people who would be willing to work to build a new reality for our people now and in the future?

Europe released its prisoners to the colonies of the New World, not only to populate the colonies, but to build a new reality from a wilderness. It worked. Australia and New Zealand were also populated by prisoners from Europe.

Twenty-five percent of our youth are in some way connected with the criminal justice system, and about half of the jails and prisons are populated by blacks. When you consider the high rate of recidivism and the cost to maintain prisoners, and when you consider that integration has not worked to advance the condition of many of our people, shouldn't we be open to new ideas, especially when they are rooted in models that have worked in the past?

Suppose we asked our brothers and sisters in Africa to carve out of that huge continent a territory for blacks from the diaspora to begin to build a new reality. Since Africans were involved in the slave trade, which brought their kith and kin to these shores in chains, thus having a hand in bringing us to our wretched present day condition, should not Africa also have a hand in our redemption? Some of our people would be willing to build a new reality on the continent of Africa, and we could do it in a way that benefits Africa, America, as well as ourselves.

The Muslims have shown a tremendous ability to reform those of our people who break the law. The movie "Malcolm X" demonstrated how the teachings of the Honorable Elijah Muhammad could reform an eighth-grade dropout student and so-called criminal into a world leader. How many future world leaders are languishing in prisons who may never have a chance to demonstrate to the world what the Almighty Creator has put in them? Our prisoners need a chance to do something constructive with their lives.

America should be willing to support the Nation of Islam for the next three or more years, to teach unhindered in the jails and prisons to begin the process of reform.

Meanwhile, we could work with African governments toward the establishment of a territorial base for our people.

There are many black scholars and professionals who are not presently working who would be willing to teach and train the inmate population in the skills necessary to build a new reality. We would offer the prisoners a chance to be reformed, trained, and then work off their time building a new reality on the African continent.

In a White House conference held nearly 130 years ago, President Abraham Lincoln tried to get blacks to go to Central America or Africa to begin a new life. He said that perhaps what we had learned in our sojourn in America would be of use to that "dark" continent. Black people turned down President Lincoln's offer and elected to stay, although the president had promised that we would never be equal in this society. President Lincoln was correct. Even to this day we are still not equal members in the society. However, since that conference, blacks have emerged as masters in every field of human endeavor. That mastery must now be put to work to lift the masses of our people in America and to help lift Africa into the 21st century.

Europe and America are attempting to get African leaders to allow them to dump their nuclear waste material on the African continent. I am not asking the government to make Africa the dumping ground for America's rejects. I am asking that America support us in first reforming the so-called criminal element among our people, and then placing them in an environment that will manifest their hidden gifts and talents.

Amends have never been made fully for the destruction of black people during the Holocaust of slavery and through the institutions of racism that have prevailed from that time to the present day. The moral issue of rectifying its role in dehumanizing an entire people still hovers over America.

In America, many of our people have been written off as members of the permanent underclass, meaning the country has lost hope in improving the condition of these people. As discussed earlier, many of our people have lost their jobs - in disproportionate numbers when compared to job loss and unemployment rates among white people - due to the deteriorating economy. This idea should be open to all of those - the permanent underclass and the unemployed - who would be interested in making a new reality for themselves on the continent of Africa.

The majority of black people will not wish to go anywhere. Because of the contributions that our forefathers have made to this land, and the contributions that blacks continue to make to America, most of our people feel that this is our only home. However, a small but significant number would be willing to try to build a new reality on the African continent, with the support of the government.

We would propose that some of the $18,000 spent each year per inmate to warehouse them in a cell be redirected to support building a new reality as outlined here. We would give the inmates a right to choose to stay here or to build a new reality in a land of their own. The freedom of choice, the right of the people to choose, has been and is the way of the teachings of the Honorable Elijah Muhammad. We have given our people an opportunity to make enlightened choices on their behalf for the past 60 years, and we will continue to do the same in the future. We would ask that the participants be granted the same dual citizenship that allows Jews to travel back and forth to Israel, making their contributions on both sides of the Atlantic.

The work done by former criminals of Europe in establishing America, New Zealand and Australia, has redeemed them in the eye of history. Let the work of the so-called underclass and so-called criminal element among black people be allowed to redeem them in the eye of history by their being permitted and supported in building a new reality on the African continent.

As Jews in America visit Israel and take pride in the accomplishments of their Jewish brothers, yet still desire to live in America, let the blacks who remain in the diaspora take pride in the work of these pioneers who would venture to build a new reality in Africa.

Further, we would establish a skills bank, composed of our scholars and professionals, for use in developing Africa and the Caribbean. We propose that these scholars and professionals work for other countries for an agreed upon compensation plan, including salary and benefits. However, what they work to develop in manufacturing, mining, agriculture and industry, a percentage of the profit would accrue to a national treasury for the benefit of those blacks who remain in America, so that on both sides of the Atlantic we will use our bitter experience for the good of Africa as well as America.

I want to briefly touch on another aspect of America's foreign relations.

Since the fall of the Soviet Union, many governments are seeking a new relationship with America. America must allow these relationships to be built on an equitable basis. This government must respect the right of self-determination for every sovereign nation.

There are nations that historically have been viewed as enemies of America. This antagonistic relationship does not necessarily have to continue. Countries like Cuba, Libya, Iran, China, Vietnam and others are all seeking to improve relations with America without compromising their dignity and self-respect.

. Imagine a world where each nation directs the focus of its energies and resources to addressing its critical internal problems that affect the quality of life of its own people, instead of focusing on meddling in the affairs of other nations.

We offer ourselves to America as an example of what can be achieved when we have the proper state of mind and connectedness with the Lord of the worlds. We can show what that Bible that many Americans have right on their shelves gathering dust can do when properly used. Although we use the Holy Qur'an, the Bible was the main tool used by the Honorable Elijah Muhammad because it was the book that we knew best. What product is America making with the Bible? We're making clean, productive black men and women from the same Bible that you read. That's our goods. That's our services.

Our people respect us. We don't go to our people with guns. We go with love and a moral imperative that appeals to their nature as the people of God.

The National Institute of Mental Health wants to say that we are genetically prone to crime. So they want to promote a drug that they say will curb crime among black people. Does America want to promote that same drug with white people, who have killed millions upon millions of blacks, native Americans, Africans, Jews, Asians and even their own Gentile brethren?

Crime is a consequence of an unjust society and a corrupt political, economic and social system. If manufacturing is brought back to the cities instead of being continually ceded to foreign countries, then we can offer our people an alternative and we can lift the poor in this country and save the cities.

When you have a relatively drug-free community you have a relatively crime-free community where the ties of family are strong and there is very little domestic violence. None of the members of the Nation of Islam are allowed to carry or possess weapons. Recently we received a contract to patrol a Los Angeles apartment complex. In just two months time the police reported that crime decreased 75%. What do we have that the police don't have? **We love our people.**

We need to promote observance of God in everything that we do. This will repair the relationships between male and female and lead to lasting, happy marriages, and the elimination of rape, incest, molestation, assault and the abuse of women. It will also repair the relationship between the governed and the governors.

It is necessary to sit and reason with us. We are ready to sit down and talk with America's leaders, if they are ready to break the mindset of a slavemaster and cancel that old master/slave relationship. We're ready to talk about instilling core values among our people, generating jobs, sacrificing to reduce the federal debt, rebuilding the cities, making the streets safer, educating our children to be the envy of the civilized world, curing AIDS, providing a future for ourselves and for all of America. Is America ready for us?

# CHAPTER
# 7

# ENDING THE HEALTH-CARE CRISIS

A t about $750 billion in spending, America spends more on health-care than any other country.[35] However, very little of this money is spent on preventive care. If America seriously hopes to end its crisis in health-care, it must redirect its attention to preventive care.

While I support a reasonable universal health-care coverage plan, making America healthy must become the personal responsibility of each citizen, and not the responsibility of government, except in those cases where preventive care is not adequate. This approach would require that each individual becomes more knowledgeable, and that leadership in the food industry, medical community and government become more responsible in providing and teaching the people the truth about caring for the human body.

## KNOWLEDGE AND VALUING
## OUR BODIES PROPERLY

The greatest gift that we have been given is the gift of life. The essence of our very being is housed within this magnificent creation of flesh and blood known as our bodies. Unfortunately, we live in a society that misdirects us and misinforms us in such a way that we place our own bodies at risk. We take care of our clothes, our pets and our material possessions better than we take care of our own bodies.

Knowledge is the principle resource that can help us take better care of our bodies and our health. God, the Creator and Sustainer of all life, has given us direction for taking care of our health. However, we live in a society that is in opposition to the directions from the Giver of life, and as a result we suffer.

It is sad that buying material possessions is valued more than getting a simple yearly checkup by a competent doctor. It is sad that watching television several hours a day takes precedence over scheduling a few minutes of exercise that would help keep our bodies and our minds fit. It is sad that we put more emphasis on going to movies and listening to music than feeding our minds through the reading of proper books and literature. And it's a tragedy that we overeat, eat the wrong foods, smoke, take drugs, drink alcohol, and take an excessive amount of pills to cope with life's stresses instead of developing the core values and self-control to protect ourselves from these addictions.

Here again, the airwaves can be used to promote a healthy lifestyle among the people.

# THE "DEATHSTYLE" OF THE AMERICAN PEOPLE

We are living relatively short lives as a result of our careless lifestyles. Sixty to 70 years is the lifespan of a typical American, and if we are fortunate to live even that short period, our lives are still riddled with every type of disease. (See Figure 7.1)

The fact is that 1/3 of all people in America will get cancer in their lifetimes, and the majority of those who do get cancer will die within a short period after diagnosis.[36] This is just one of the many sad facts resulting from our lack of knowledge and general disrespect of life.

According to the Bible, we live in a world that is called "death." The lifestyles of the people reflect this world of death. This world of death is caused by rebellion against Allah, God, who is the source of good and life.

The lifestyles of the people reflect this world of death. In Proverbs it reads, *"There is a way which seemeth right unto a man, but the ends thereof are the ways of death."* (Proverbs 14:12) Most of us believe our lifestyles are correct, and we have prided ourselves in the lifestyles we live no matter how degenerate they may be according to the standard raised by Almighty God.

*Health United States 1990*, published by the U.S. Department of Health and Human Services, provides statistics which clearly illustrate that the lifestyles of the American people pave the way toward early and unnecessary death.

# Figure 7.1: Life Expectancy Rates

| | **Males** | | **Females** | |
|---|---|---|---|---|
| Rank | Country | Years | Country | Years |
| 1 | Japan | 75.9 | Japan | 82.1 |
| 2 | Sweden | 74.2 | France | 81.1 |
| 3 | Hong Kong | 74.2 | Switzerland | 81.0 |
| 4 | Greece | 74.1 | Sweden | 80.4 |
| 5 | Switzerland | 74.0 | Netherlands | 80.3 |
| 6 | Netherlands | 73.6 | Canada | 80.2 |
| 7 | Israel | 73.4 | Australia | 79.8 |
| 8 | Canada | 73.3 | Norway | 79.8 |
| 9 | Australia | 73.2 | Hong Kong | 79.7 |
| 10 | Spain | 73.1 | Spain | 79.7 |
| 11 | Cuba | 73.0 | Italy | 79.2 |
| 12 | Norway | 72.8 | Greece | 78.9 |
| 13 | Italy | 72.7 | Finland | 78.9 |
| 14 | England & Wales | 72.6 | Germany (Federal) | 78.9 |
| 15 | France | 72.6 | Puerto Rico | 78.9 |
| | | | *United States - Whites* | *78.9* |
| 16 | Kuwait | 72.5 | *United States - Total* | *78.4* |
| | *United States - Whites* | *72.3* | | |
| 17 | Germany (Federal) | 72.2 | England & Wales | 78.3 |
| 18 | Costa Rica | 72.1 | Austria | 78.2 |
| 19 | Denmark | 71.9 | Belgium | 78.2 |
| 20 | Ireland | 71.6 | Denmark | 78.0 |
| 21 | Austria | 71.6 | Portugal | 77.5 |
| 22 | *United States - Total* | *71.5* | New Zealand | 77.3 |
| 23 | Belgium | 71.4 | Ireland | 77.3 |
| 24 | Singapore | 71.3 | Northern Ireland | 77.2 |
| 25 | Northern Ireland | 71.1 | Israel | 77.0 |
| 26 | New Zealand | 71.0 | Costa Rica | 76.9 |
| 27 | Puerto Rico | 70.7 | Scotland | 76.6 |
| 28 | Finland | 70.7 | Singapore | 76.5 |
| 29 | Portugal | 70.6 | Cuba | 76.5 |
| 30 | Scotland | 70.5 | Germany (Democratic) | 76.0 |
| 31 | Chile | 70.0 | Kuwait | 75.8 |
| 32 | Germany (Democratic) | 69.9 | Chile | 75.7 |
| 33 | Yugoslavia | 68.5 | Czechoslovakia | 75.3 |
| 34 | Bulgaria | 68.3 | Poland | 75.2 |
| 35 | Czechoslovakia | 67.7 | Bulgaria | 74.6 |
| 36 | Romania | 67.1 | Yugoslaavia | 74.3 |
| 37 | Poland | 66.8 | Hungary | 73.9 |
| 38 | Hungary | 65.7 | U.S.S.R. | 73.9 |
| | | | *United States - Blacks* | *73.4* |
| 39 | U.S.S.R. | 65.1 | Romania | 72.7 |
| | *United States - Blacks* | *64.9* | | |

Source: U.S. Department of Health and Human Services, 1990

Of all the countries in the world the life expectancy of the American people, in a land of power and plenty, ranks 16th for women and 22nd for men. Japan ranks first for both sexes. This is a shame. U.S. citizens, male and female, live only 60-70 years, and blacks trail whites in life expectancy across both sexes. So if America is 16th for women and 22nd for men, and as black men and women we trail further behind them, then as a people in a land of power and plenty blacks are in a condition virtually no better than the worst Third World countries in terms of health and longevity.

Two million Americans lose their lives each year, and more than 250,000 of those deaths are among black people. Our death rates are disproportionate when compared with those of whites across most of the leading causes of death.

The leading causes of death for blacks and whites are: heart disease, cancer, hypertension and cerebrovascular disease, accidents, homicide and legal intervention, pneumonia and influenza, diabetes, lung disease, AIDS, cirrhosis and liver disease, and suicide. (See Figure 7.2)

About half of all deaths, or a million lives each year, are accounted for by heart disease and cancer. In every different cause of death, the death rate for blacks is on average about 55% greater than death rates for whites.

The No. 1 killer for all Americans is heart disease. The death rate from heart disease is 30% to 60% greater for blacks than for whites, with heart disease claiming nearly 100,000 black lives each year. I would propose that the high level of heart disease is in part the body's response to stress from America's loss of power and prestige in the world, and particularly the decline of

# Figure 7.2:
# Leading Causes of Death

| Rank | Cause | Total Number of Deaths | Black Deaths |
|---|---|---|---|
| 1 | Heart Disease | 765,156 | 79,466 |
| 2 | Cancer | 485,048 | 53,968 |
| 3 | Hypertension & Cerebrovascular Disease | 150,517 | 18,479 |
| 4 | Accidents | 97,100 | 13,487 |
| 5 | Lung Disease | 82,853 | 5,476 |
| 6 | Pneumonia & Influenza | 77,662 | 7,191 |
| 7 | Diabetes | 40,368 | 6,972 |
| 8 | Suicide | 30,407 | 2,022 |
| 9 | Cirrhosis & Liver Disease | 26,409 | 3,903 |
| 10 | Homicide & Legal Intervention | 22,032 | 10,403 |
| 11 | AIDS | 16,602 | 5,197 |
| 12 | Other | 373,845 | 57,455 |
| | All Causes | 2,167,999 | 264,019 |

Source: U.S. Department of Health and Human Services, 1990. Data from 1988.

America's economy. I would also propose that the high level of heart disease among black people, in part reflects the inordinate degree of stress due to the pervasive racism that we live under each day. These propositions are exactly in accord with the scriptures wherein it reads, *"And there shall be signs in the sun, and in the moon, and in the stars; and upon the earth distress of nations, with perplexity; the sea and the waves roaring, men's hearts failing them for fear, and for looking after those things which are coming on the earth..."* (Luke 21:25-26)

Approximately one million people develop cancer each year, and 1,350 die each day from some form of the disease. As with most causes of death, the death rate for cancer is highest among black males, whose rate is 44% higher than white males. The leading type of cancer for males is prostate cancer, with new incidences 30% higher among black males than among whites.

Overall, black women die from cancer at a rate 19% greater than white women. However the rate of new incidences of cancer are actually higher for white women. Women are particularly vulnerable to breast cancer, with incidences among whites 16% higher than for blacks.

Rates of death for hypertension and cerebrovascular diseases, diabetes, pneumonia and influenza, cirrhosis and liver disease, all are higher for blacks, particularly black men. In fact the death rate for black males is nearly double that of white males for these diseases.

Most dramatic is the disproportionate number of black males who die as a result of homicide and police intervention. Twenty-five to 40 black men are killed and murdered each day, which is more than the total number of white men who are either killed or murdered each day. A black man is seven times more likely to die from street violence, including confrontations with the police, than a white man.

Even among women, blacks are four times more likely to die from street violence than whites. And street violence is the No. 1 killer of young black adults ages 15-44. Approximately 59,000 American soldiers died in the nine years of fighting in Vietnam. It is said that 35% of those deaths, or about 20,000 of the casualties were black. But each year over 10,000 blacks lose their lives to street violence. So in the same nine-year period we lost nearly five times as many black lives in the streets of America as in Vietnam. This would suggest it's safer to grow up in a war zone than it is in the inner cities of America.

We could easily conclude from these statistics that all of our lives are in peril, and deeper, we could conclude that there is an assault on the black male. The black male is walking more deeply into the valley of the shadow of death than any other member of American society, which means that black women are more frequently becoming widows and without their male counterparts.

When we consider the number of black men incarcerated, jobless or on drugs, there is no wonder that there already exists a preponderance of females in the population over that of males. If the trend in black male death rates is not reversed, the black male will soon be extinct, and the black female will be left as prey in the hands of men who do not love her, and only wish to continue to use her.

As many of you know, AIDS takes its greatest death toll on blacks. Black men are three times more likely to die from AIDS than white men, and black women are six times more likely to die from AIDS than white women. At present, blacks make up 25% of all AIDS cases, and black children make up an alarmingly high rate of 50% of children's cases of AIDS.

As odd as it may sound, suicide is the one leading cause of death that is dominated by whites. Nearly 30,000 whites take their lives each year compared with 2,000 Blacks. More whites die from suicide than from AIDS.

About 40,000 babies are lost each year due to infant mortality. Again 25% of the deaths are black babies. The infant mortality rate for blacks is about double that of whites, and is largely due to low birthweights. Low birthweights and the resulting infant mortality could be prevented if prospective mothers adopted better eating habits and better lifestyles and were diligent about pre-natal care. Only about 60% of black mothers get ade-quate prenatal care compared to 80% of white mothers.

Again, you can see from these statistics compiled by the U.S. Department of Health and Human Services, that we are living in the valley of the shadow of death. Many of us have no health insurance and no dental plan. We do not even have the knowledge of preventive care, which would lessen the importance of our having insurance. Thirty-six million Americans are walking the streets without health insurance. Only 60% of blacks have private health insurance compared to 80% of whites, and as jobs continue to be lost, health insurance benefits will be lost as well. (See Figure 7.3)

So we are suffering, and in terms of health the only way we can come out of this is with the proper use of knowledge that will allow us to prevent 90% of the sicknesses that we are dying from.

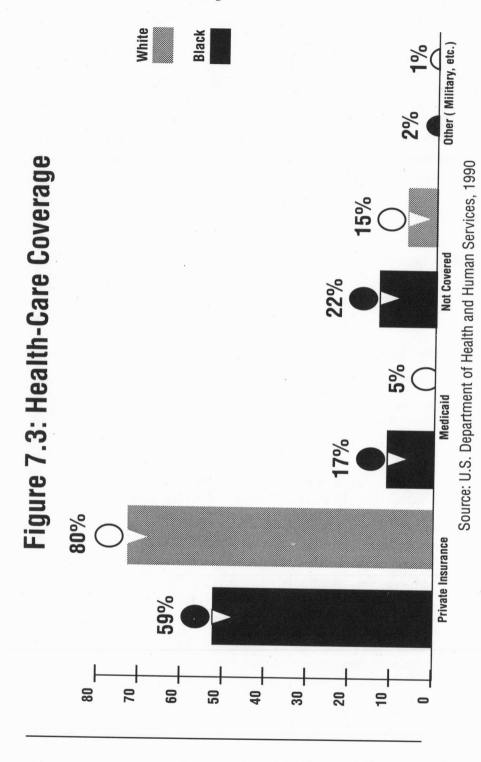

Figure 7.3: Health-Care Coverage

Source: U.S. Department of Health and Human Services, 1990

We need to understand that we have been trained in a self-destructive way of behavior and that we are caught up in a vicious cycle of death. Our lifestyle is really a deathstyle. We all have to die. This is assured. But our time of death in most cases reflects the personal decisions of each individual. The Bible teaches that the wages of sin is death, and as long as we pursue the ways of this world, wrong over right, falsehood over truth, wealth over health, we will pay the price.

Look at how degenerate the society has become. One-third of the teenage and adult population smokes, and black males are smoking in the highest proportions, nearly 40%. (See Figure 7.4) On the cigarette package it warns that smoking is dangerous to your health. In fact, 87% of lung disease, a major killer, is due to smoking, according to the National Cancer Institute.

Smoking is a worldwide phenomenon, particularly among Third World people. In my travels throughout the world I have witnessed little children smoking American-made cigarettes. As the market in America dries up - due to more knowledge of the devastating effects of smoking - the tobacco industry floods the Third World and targets the black community with these habit-forming instruments of death. With predatory practices like this, it should be no wonder why people in foreign lands, particularly Africa and the Middle East, proclaim America as the "great Shaitan," or Satan.

Food addiction and the eating of improper foods has one quarter of Americans overweight. Black women are in the worst condition as nearly half of them are overweight. (See Figure 7.5) Our weight problem is the result of eating too much food and eating the wrong foods. Uninformed eating habits has us buying and liv-

# Figure 7.4: Smoking by Race and Sex

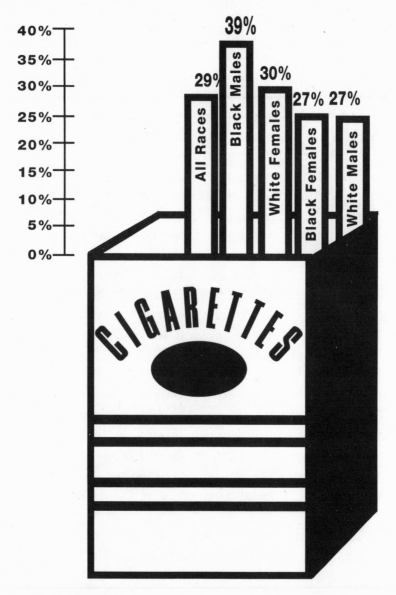

Source : U.S. Department of Health and Human Services, 1990

ing off unhealthy, high-fat, high-cholesterol, and low-fiber diets that completely destroy our appearance. Thirty percent of the population has high cholesterol, which leads to heart disease and cancer, especially colon and rectal cancer.

Half of what we eat is eaten out, predominantly at fast food chains that advertise heavily to drive the purchase of overly processed foods. Advertisers often use our most gifted athletes to get us to buy death burgers, with their additives, pork, bleached bread, hormones and preservatives. And we buy it and eat it and get fatter and sicker and poorer each day from doctor bills we can't afford to pay, and from buying pills for acid indigestion and heartburn and headaches, all due to the toxins that get stored in our bodies from the overly processed and improper foods that we eat.

Fifty percent of the population has high blood pressure and hypertension, which are the leading causes of 500,000 strokes each year and major contributors to heart attacks. High blood pressure and hypertension are again the result of, eating fried, salty, sugary foods, and a lack of exercise.

What we are witnessing is that fast food equals fast death. And a sedentary lifestyle, meaning a lifestyle where you just sit as a couch potato observing the television, or work in a stationary position, getting no form of exercise, gets you an early seat in the grave.

Now I don't know about you, but I would certainly like to stay out of the grave since we're going to be in the grave for such a long time. Wouldn't you like to prolong your life? Then someone has to inspire you to change your way of living.

Did you know that the simple, cost-you-nothing things like prayer, proper rest, proper diet and fasting

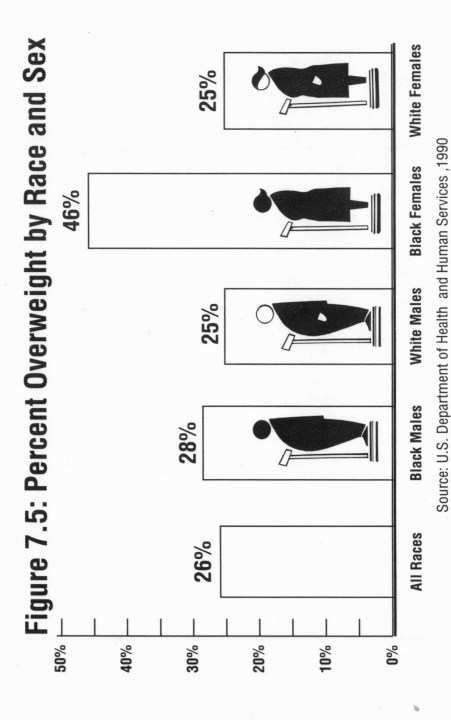

Figure 7.5: Percent Overweight by Race and Sex

Source: U.S. Department of Health and Human Services, 1990

can help heal whatever ails you? The Honorable Elijah Muhammad taught that 90% of our illnesses could be cured by just fasting. Proper rest, proper diet and fasting can help the body heal itself of toxins, especially those caused by stress. But do we rest properly? Do we fast? Do we have a proper diet? Do we maintain a connection with the Divine Being through prayer? No. Instead we engage in riotous behavior and we have moved away from God in a very extreme way, leading us many steps closer to the grave.

Promiscuity and homosexual sex and the use of intravenous drugs is causing us to have AIDS and a host of other sexually transmitted diseases. Drinking alcoholic beverages is giving us cirrhosis and other liver disease, and leads to the majority of motor vehicle accidents. There's virtually a liquor store and a liquor billboard advertisement on every corner in the most impoverished inner-city communities. And nearby there is often a church. So after you drink yourself to death, quite conveniently, there is the church and the good reverend to bury you. And the reverend will probably say at your funeral how God called you home, when really it was the liquor merchants and your unwillingness to say no to their advertisements that led you into disease and ultimately into an early grave. A great deal of this way of life is created for us by what could be called the "merchants of death."

## THE MERCHANTS OF DEATH

There's tremendous profit in promoting the death-dealing lifestyles that many of us lead. You may not believe it but the leading promoters of our destructive lifestyles are the United States government, the food and drug industries and the medical community.

According to the Rand Corporation, in a statement published in the *Journal of the American Medical Association*, "one-fourth of hospital days, one-fourth of procedures, and two-fifths of medications could be done without."[37] I want you to think about this. Because it should be no secret that when there's a profit to be made, regardless to its adverse effects on human life, there are always those who will choose wealth over the health of the American people.

Medical care is big business. Three quarters of a trillion dollars, or 12% of the gross national product of this country is spent on health care expenditures.

In many respects America has become a pill society. Billions are spent each year on over-the-counter drugs. Americans spend $1.5 billion a year on cholesterol-lowering drugs instead of eating properly.[38] Merchants of death have a vested interest in keeping you ignorant and perpetually sick.

Over $160 billion is spent each year on cancer and heart disease treatments, and there is no guarantee that with surgery or with another of the various forms of treatment you'll be free of the disease.[39] Treatments, including surgery, tend to further traumatize the body and depress the body's immunological systems. For example, one of the treatments of cancer is chemotherapy. Chemotherapy is literally germ warfare on the body. The treatment is a by-product of W.W.II chemical and biological warfare research. Chemotherapy works by attacking cells within the body, killing normal cells in its efforts to kill the cancerous cells. The result is a weakened body with no guarantee that you are cured of cancer. I am only pointing out the disadvantages of current treatments. I am not suggesting that you should not take the treatments prescribed by your doctor when your cancer or disease has progressed so far along that surgery or chemotherapy is the only option available.

The food industry is a $400 billion industry, based on promoting death-dealing overly processed foods.[40] America's diet of three meals a day with three snacks in between each meal is unhealthy. It is unhealthy because it consists largely of fast food and food that is overly processed in America's food factories. The foods get defibered, degerminated, defatted, refatted, and manipulated in countless ways other than how food is intended for us to eat. It's no coincidence that the first heart attack reported in America was in 1896, the same time our diets began changing from a rural-based local supply of food to the national food supply chains of highly processed foods.[41]

It is now being proven by scientists that what the Honorable Elijah Muhammad taught on how to eat to live - one meal a day, no snacks in between meals, and to eat only the best foods - is absolutely correct and good for the body.

By our not having the knowledge of chemistry, we do not understand the effects from how the food industry injects hormones into chickens, beef, lamb and pork to fatten these animals up to get them to the market quicker to make a quicker dollar. We do not understand that as we ingest these meats, our bodies react to the hormones. As a result, our girls at 9 are developing breasts and having their menses. Our young men are prematurely developing sexually. These hormones stimulate sexual development. When you add this to the degenerative kind of display of nakedness and filth in movies, television, songs, books and magazines, no wonder teenage sex and teenage pregnancy and teenage violence is greater now than it ever was. This is a vicious circle of death dealing for the sake of profit. And who is the loser? The American people, especially black people and particularly black men.

How do we break this vicious cycle? How do we get out of this cycle of death? First, we must go back to Him who gave us the gift of life and Who is the Best Knower of how to protect, develop and properly care for and nurture the life that he has given. And that is Allah (God), the Creator Himself.

It's interesting that when you go out and buy something - something for your hair, a new cassette player, a cake mix - in the box or on the jar there are directions for proper use. When you buy clothing you will find on the tag somewhere directions for how to clean it properly to avoid ruining the garment. If you value what you have purchased, you study the directions and you follow them to the best of your ability. Isn't it sad that with life we don't follow the directions for how to use it, take care of it, and help our lives evolve in a proper manner?

Those directions for life are in the scriptures brought by the Prophets. But they are buried under teachings that make us comfortable in getting ready to live in another world after death rather than preparing us for the life and the problems in life that we are confronting right now.

I've often noticed how people go into houses of God with such reverence. I have visited Mecca several times and I have visited Al-Harem, which is the sacred house of all Muslims, and I watched the way each Muslim approached that house, as I did, with great reverence. Of course the house is a house made of stone. I have visited St. Peter's Basilica and I watched the reverence with which Catholics and visitors approached that magnificent structure. I've watched the dedication of religious houses and I see how spiritually-minded people act in a religous house. They are quiet in their decorum and they will not utter certain words. They try to be very respectful around the altar. But all of these buildings are the work of the hands of men, while the human body is the handiwork of God Himself. It bothers me that we would show more respect for a house of stone built by men and designed by men in their vanity, and yet be so disrespectful of the true house of God designed by the Supreme Architect of all creation.

Don't you think that we ought to change our focus and become more respectful of the human body as the true house of the living God? There is no house on earth more holy than this wonderful magnificent structure created by the Lord of the worlds. We ought to clean it up.

Most of our sickness can be traced to our rebellion against Divine law. Look in your Bible. Look at the old patriarchs. Read how long they lived. If you believe the bible to be a true account of the lives of these men, then 400, 500, 600, 700, 800, nearly 1,000 years is the lifespan of these men.

The Honorable Elijah Muhammad taught us that if we learned how to live properly, we could extend our days to 200, to 300 and 400 years. If we taught our children how to respect their lives, maybe three or four generations from now our children would learn how to live 500 to 1,000 years of age. This is what is meant in the scripture that we would live as trees. There are trees that have been on this earth over 1,000 years. And yet we, the greatest of God's creations, cannot make it to 60 or 70 years old without being stricken by death or a debilitating disease.

If you love yourself and you love your children and your grandchildren, then you ought to make a change now. As young people, don't wait until you're old to make a change. The time to change the style that is leading to death is now, before you bring forth new life onto this earth.

The desire to change must come before change can come. Desire must feed the will, and the will of the human being is what empowers us to make the change. It is written in the Holy Qur'an that Allah, God, will never change the condition of a people until they change what is in themselves. So the burden is not on God to change us. The burden is on us to change when knowledge comes that dictates that we must change. Then we must develop the will to change. There's a saying that nothing is more powerful than a made-up mind. If you are ready to choose health, then health can come to you.

Prayer will strengthen the will. Prayer will constantly feed the desire. Desire will feed the will, and once the will is strong enough, you can change.

One doctor lamented that, "Your doctor will tell you to lose weight, stop smoking, exercise more and relax, but he doesn't have the time or the know-how to give you the tools to make the changes. So you continue the same unhealthy lifestyle as before and, naturally when you return for your next doctor's visit, your blood pressure hasn't come down. So the doctor has no choice but to start drug treatment or increase medication."[42] Sometimes this is because the doctor is the victim of the very thing the doctor is treating you for. In fact, many times the doctors are as sickly as their patients and die just as young.

Do you want to make the change? Yes, you say. But you ask, how do I do it? And the answer is, **just do it!** One day a young sister who had a problem with smoking wrote the Honorable Elijah Muhammad and asked him, "Dear apostle, how can I stop smoking?", and the Honorable Elijah Muhammad wrote her back and he said, "Dear sister, If you desire to stop smoking, stop. Best wishes for your continued success, I am, Your brother and servant, Elijah Muhammad." She brought me the letter and she was quite upset that he only told her to "stop."

What was he saying to this sister that she didn't understand? He was saying to her, "**you** have the power to stop". Use your will and say I **won't** do it anymore and then **don't** do it anymore.

There is a scripture in the Bible about a woman Jesus met who was possessed of seven devils. Jesus cast the devils out of this woman, and as the devils were coming out they rebuked Jesus for casting them out, what they thought, ahead of time. They knew that the work of Jesus was to cast out devils, but they thought they had a longer time to inhabit the woman. They were coming out but they were angry as they were coming out and they were giving Jesus a hard way to go.

When Jesus comes into the world he comes to heal the people of Satan's work. He comes to restore us to health and well-being. He comes to reconcile man with the divinity of his own nature. He comes to reconcile man with God. We all are possessed of devils. Each of us is possessed of these seven devils and seven devils only means the tremendous powers of evil that are absolutely destroying our lives. What we want you to do is make up your minds to cast seven devils out of self. Make up your minds to adopt a new life with the ever-presence of truth and God.

The first devil you have to cast out is ignorance. The Bible teaches, "*My people are destroyed for the lack of knowledge...*" (Hosea 4:6) Ignorance is the No. 1 destroyer of the human family.

Another devil right along with ignorance is pride. You are proud of your ignorance, therefore truth cannot come to free you of your ignorance, because pride stands in the way of your receiving the truth. Pride keeps your ears from opening that your heart may receive the truth. And even though Jesus said you shall know the truth and the truth shall make you free, he also said that it is the organ of hearing that allows you to receive the truth. He that hath ears let him hear. It is precisely this organ of hearing you must use now to hear the truth and obey the directions that are good for your life, your body and spirit.

Once we get rid of ignorance and pride, we must work on getting rid of arrogance, greed, avarice, lust and selfishness. Then, on the physical level, we must stop eating pork. We must stop drinking alcohol, using tobacco, drugs, and we must stop eating a host of other bad food. These are all little devils that we must drive out of ourselves.

According to the Bible and the Qur'an, the eating of swine is forbidden. (Leviticus 11:7) The Honorable Elijah Muhammad writes, in *How To Eat To Live*, that the pig is "the foulest of animals. It is so poisonous that you can hardly poison it with other poisons. It is so poisonous and filthy that nature had to prepare it with a sewer line and you may find the opening on its forelegs. It is a little hole out of which pus oozes. Its poison is that of a live nature, in the form of a parasitic worm that is called trichina."[43] This is why, as some say, pork has to be cured. But it can never be cured. It is a foul and poisonous animal that is infested with worms and pus, the eating of which destroys the beauty of the body's appearance and turns the body into a house of filth, vulnerable to every manner of disease.

Just look at the appearance of those who eat a lot of pork and observe how they act. Remember, you are what you eat. The only reason our people came to eat pork was because during slavery this was the only meat the slavemaster would give us to eat. The slavemaster would give us the worst pieces of the hog, the intestines, the feet, the snout and the tail. This filthy practice became the main dish in what is now called soul food. We are destroyed for our lack of knowledge and our rebellion against the will of God.

## PREVENTIVE CARE GUIDELINES

If you have the desire, then you need to develop the will and gain the know-how to cast these seven devils out. Simply follow these eight guidelines.

**First**, you must pray. You must let the Author of all existence into your life. As I said earlier, it's prayer that feeds and strengthens your desire, and desire feeds the will. Your will gives you the strength to cast out the seven devils and to begin to build yourself into a house fit for the habitation of God.

**Second**, you must imbue yourself with knowledge. You need knowledge. You must not take pride in what you think you already know. Just look at your self-destructive behavior. It is a sufficient witness against what you think you know, for if you knew better you would do better. As the scripture teaches, "...*become as little children...*" (Matthew 18:3) then you can more easily accept the knowledge that will prepare a kingdom of heaven for you right on this Earth, and get you out of the valley of death.

In fact the book that has made me a healthier individual is *How To Eat To Live,* Books I & II by the Honorable Elijah Muhammad. You can get a copy at the local mosque of the Nation of Islam. Also, get your subscription to *The Final Call* newspaper and read the articles on health. Again, your local mosque will have *The Final Call* as well as the *Muslim Cookbook* which will help you prepare meals that are easy on the budget and good for your family's health.

Go to your library and read the books on health. Go to your store and get a copy of some of the health magazines like *Prevention, Health, HealthQuest* and *Vegetarian Times.*

**Third,** strive to eat to live instead of eating inordinately and improperly in an attempt to deal with stress or to entertain yourself. The Surgeon General's report on Nutrition and Health says that diet-related diseases account for 68% of all deaths in this country. How we are eating is literally killing us - killing us outwardly in terms of obesity and poor physical appearance; killing us from the inside in the form of disease. So we need to not glory in fat, but to see fat as an enemy. We need to declare war on fat. We especially need to declare war on eating pork, which does no good for us. Eating pork accumulates swill in the body, particularly the blood stream, and therefore it equals death.

Our kitchens and our food purchase decisions can replace the doctor's office. Did you know that fewer than 10% of Americans are getting the minimum amount of fruit and vegetables, according to the *American Journal of Public Health?* And did you know that according to the National Center for Disease Control 25% of low-income blacks suffer from linear growth retardation resulting from malnutrition?

We must eat to live and declare war on fat and malnutrition.

**Fourth,** we must exercise. If you can afford it, get one of the inexpensive memberships in a health club and workout on a regular basis. If you cannot afford a health club membership, then do some form of exercise right in your home. In consultation with a trained physical instructor, you should develop a fitness program that is right for you. At a minimum, walking a few miles each day is one of the best forms of exercise.

**Fifth,** get rid of your addictions. That is drugs, alcohol, smoking and extra-marital sex. Many of us have a problem just saying no. In Islam, the religion of submission to the will of God, fasting is prescribed as a way to cleanse the body but also as a means of fortifying the will. When we fast we fast for a minimum of three days without eating. Eating is such a natural thing for us to do. But when we can control ourselves to forego what is natural for us to do, this makes it so much easier to get rid of things we should not be doing and that are harmful to the body. This is a prescription from the Supreme Being. So try fasting as a way to build your will so that you can rid yourself of addictions before your addictions rid the Earth of you.

**Sixth,** get proper rest and relaxation. Allow your body time to recuperate from the emotional stress and physical exertion of the day, and to re-energize itself to meet the challenges of the next day. Relax yourself by breaking your daily routine with some joyful activity that frees your mind of life's stresses and strains. Some enjoy a game of golf. Many have hobbies or crafts as outlets for expressing their own creativity. For others cooking can be very relaxing. I play the violin, an instrument I haven't practiced or played for nearly 40 years, to take my mind away from the stresses of my daily routine.

**Seventh**, you should spend a little time in the sun and communing with nature. Too much sun is not good for you. But limited exposure to the sun is good for the body. The sun is the source of life, light and energy. It emits vitamin-filled rays that are absorbed through the skin, helping the body to defend itself against disease.

**Eighth** and finally, you should make sure that you and your family get regular dental and physical check-ups.

Some of you may still think that living healthy lives is either vain or foolish. You may feel that these simple guidelines for healthful living are too restricting and don't leave you free to enjoy life. I challenge you to think about how restricting life already is. I'd say that one-third of us getting cancer is pretty restricting by itself. Think about how restricting lung disease is. Think about how restricting it is to lose the use of your limbs due to the crippling effects of a stroke.

Beyond preventing disease and cutting this country's health-care bill, black people in particular have even more reason to make a change and adopt healthful living as a priority.

We already know we live in a racist society. But did you know that the very stress of racism cripples us in a way that leaves us susceptible to illnesses and lifestyles that lead to illnesses and death? The constant ever-presence of racism in every aspect of our lives triggers physiological responses that release hormones into the body that can harm us.

One leading doctor, Dr. John L. Mason, wrote in his book *Guide to Stress Reduction,* that "if a stress response is chronic, the constant presence of stress hormones begins to wear down the body's immunological systems."[44] The stress from the constant bombardment of racism, from our being in America under this system of hatred toward black people, works to increase the heartbeat, tense the muscles, increase the blood pressure and ultimately release adrenaline and other hormones into the body. Without a physical outlet to free you of the buildup of these hormones and adrenaline, these things wear down the immunological systems and leave you vulnerable to illness and disease. Or, you begin to seek mood-altering substances like drugs, alcohol, food, or even sex or violence to help make you feel better. After we destroy ourselves, through our response to the destructive enemy assault of racism, we then look to the doctor or the government to help us.

Let me remind you, the key to solving our problems begins with self-improvement. The government and the medical community cannot be relied on to solve our problems. Take cancer as an example. When former President Nixon launched the National Cancer Act in 1971, he funded the National Cancer Institute with a $1.4 billion annual budget.[45] Since that time there has been no marked improvement in cancer death rates. All we've received is warnings that smoking, improper diet, lack of exercise, getting an annual checkup, all of these simple guidelines to healthful living can dramatically reduce the risk of cancer. $1.4 billion for each of the past 20 years amounts to $28 billion. That's taxpayers money that could have been left in our pockets or used to create jobs for the unemployed, not for some doctor at the National Cancer Institute to come tell you not to smoke.

The fact is the government does not appear to be genuinely interested in the well-being of the American people. Of course, the jury is still out on the present administration. Mrs. Hillary Clinton at least appears concerned about health issues.

However, according to the Public Health Service, given the excessive deaths in the Black community, the government has written off the possibility of closing the gap in the near future. And if we are written off in the near future, then what future is there in continuing to look to the government for help? We must now look to God and ourselves for solutions to our problems.

The route to economic and political empowerment begins with affirming the Will of God and living in accord with His directions. Why would we add poor health to a condition that is already economically, socially and politically disadvantaged? We compound our own disadvantage by partaking of the slough-trough of the degenerate life of America's popular culture instead of raising ourselves up and being a beacon of hope and an example to every oppressed group of people on the earth.

We need a healthy community to shoulder the responsibility of self-determination. You cannot fight for self-determination when you are at war with your own body and mind.

I'm urging you to adopt healthy lifestyles, not for vanity's sake, but for the sake of our future, and our grandchildren's future. Because without healthy, strong bodies, wise and disciplined minds, we only help the enemy by serving as the instruments of our own extinction.

# CHAPTER

# 8

# A VISION FOR AMERICA

Nineteen ninety-two marked the quincenten-
nial year of the opening up of the "New
World" for the purpose of Western domina-
tion. Christopher Columbus is said to have "discovered" this continent in 1492. Since 1492 the Native
American people have been misused, abused and then
neglected. Since 1555, the black people brought to
these shores in chains have also been misused, abused
and now remain neglected.

In the official History of the Seal of the United
States, published by the Department of State in 1909,
Gaillard Hunt wrote that late in the afternoon of July 4,
1776, The Continental Congress resolved that Dr.
Benjamin Franklin, Mr. John Adams and Mr. Thomas
Jefferson be a committee to prepare a device for a Seal

of the United States of America. In the design proposed by the first committee, the obverse (face) of the Seal was a coat of arms in six quarters, with emblems representing England, Scotland, Ireland, France, Germany and Holland, the countries from which the new nation had been peopled. The Eye of Providence in a radiant triangle, and the motto E PLURIBUS UNUM were also proposed for the obverse.[46]

Even though the country was populated by so-called Indians, and black slaves were brought to build the country, the official Seal of the country was never designed to reflect our presence, only that of the European immigrants. The Seal and the Constitution reflect the thinking of the founding fathers that this was to be a nation by white people and for white people. Native Americans, blacks and all other non-white people were to be the burden bearers for the "real" citizens of this nation.

For the reverse (back) of the Seal, the committee suggested a picture of Pharaoh sitting in an open chariot with a crown on his head and a sword in his hand, passing through the divided waters of the Red Sea in pursuit of the Israelites. Hovering over the sea was to be shown a pillar of fire in a cloud, expressive of the Divine presence and command. Rays from this pillar of fire were to be shown beaming on Moses, standing on the shore and extending his hand over the sea, causing it to overwhelm Pharaoh. The motto for the reverse was: REBELLION TO TYRANTS IS OBEDIENCE TO GOD.

The design reveals the spiritual blindness inherent in the genesis of the United States. The founding fathers upheld obedience to God as their symbol while practicing genocide, colonialism and slavery among the native population and our forebears.

It was Thomas Jefferson who said, "I tremble for my country when I reflect that God is just and that His justice cannot sleep forever." It was George Washington who said that he feared the slaves would become a most troublesome species of property before too many years passed over our heads.

America is faced with the political and moral dilemma of reconciling pluralism and the inclusion of non-whites with the democratic ideas espoused by the founding fathers. This is not a democracy in the fullest meaning of the word. Racism has to be overcome in order to gain a full expression of E Pluribus Unum (out of the many, one). Is E Pluribus Unum meant to be interpreted as "out of the many white ethnic strains, one people," or "out of the many strains, white, black and other, one people?"

Within the walls of this country there are two Americas, separate and unequal, white and black (including other non-whites). In order to reconcile these two Americas, the American people must come to terms with the limited vision of the founding fathers. The founding fathers didn't envision the current population profile, where the numbers of black and Hispanic people are growing, threatening the majority status of whites. Those who desire to maintain the old vision of white rule under the name of democracy and pluralism will no longer be able to continue the subjugation of non-whites. Now is the time for freedom, justice and equality for those who have been deprived of it.

It was made easy for whites to subjugate others because they were taught to see blacks and Native

Americans as heathen, savage and sub-human. This, in their minds, justified their not recognizing us as equal citizens in this country. Bearing this in mind, that the original Seal should include a picture of Pharaoh pursuing the Israelites is not without great significance. That it should include a pillar of fire in a cloud, beaming down on Moses, is not without significance for this day and time.

In my judgment, the original Seal was inspired to give America a picture of what her future could become if she did not do justice by the Native Americans and by the blacks who were brought here as her slaves.

Even though America says she wants change and renewal, she must deal with the basis of this country's woes. Either she must evolve from the limited vision of the founding fathers and repudiate that vision, or, America must say that she believes in the true vision of the founding fathers and that the darker people will never be respected as equals inside of this nation.

God has set His hand against this economy as He set His hand against the riches of Egypt. **The only way to fix this economy is to deal with greed, basic immorality and the unwanted presence of 30 million or more black people and 2 million Native Americans whose cry for justice has entered the ears of God.**

Integration, as it has been conceived, is not working to bring true freedom, justice and equality to America's former slaves. It is not working because it was not properly motivated and is not in harmony with the mandate of the time.

We do not want or need that kind of integration that literally results in nothing in terms of economic advancement for our people. The Honorable Elijah Muhammad said that if we wanted better relations between black and white, he could show us how to achieve this. As black people, we first have to come into a knowledge of self that will help us make ourselves worthy of respect and our communities decent places in which to live. We must begin to do something for self. This act on our part will earn the respect of self as well as others. It will ultimately help us to have better relations with those who see us as an unwanted burden in this society.

The focus of black people should be on elevating self, not on trying to force ourselves into the communities of white people. Self-respecting white men do not want to see us with their women. One way to have good race relations is to leave their women and girls alone. Some of us have a false love for the white woman, and some of us have a false love for the white man. Some want the former slavemaster's woman because the former slavemaster has always had free access to our women, and some want the white man because he wields great power in the society.

In a painful recount of the position our freed forebears found themselves in after Emancipation, W.E.B. DuBois wrote:

"*For the first time he sought to analyze the burden he bore upon his back, that dead-weight of social degradation partially masked behind a half-named Negro problem. He felt his poverty; without a cent, without a home, without land, tools, or savings, he had entered into competition with rich, landed, skilled neighbors. To be a poor man is hard, but to be a poor race in a land of dollars is the very bottom of hardships. He felt the weight of his ignorance, not simply of letters, but of life, of business, of the humanities; the accumulated sloth and shirking and awkwardness of decades and centuries shackled his hands and feet. Nor was his burden all poverty and ignorance. The red stain of bastardy, which two centuries of systematic legal defilement of Negro women had stamped upon his race, meant not only the loss of ancient African chastity, but also the hereditary weight of a mass of corruption from white adulterers, threatening almost the obliteration of the Negro home."* [47]

At one time, white folks held up the Cadillac as the symbol of success. We who were not successful, wanted to at least have the symbol of success, so we aspired to own a Cadillac. Likewise, white men have held up white women as the best and most beautiful women on the Earth. To have a loving relationship with her - to marry her or to have sex with her - to many of our black men is the epitome of being accepted and successful.

The Honorable Elijah Muhammad taught us to take our own women and girls and respect, honor and protect them. He taught us to work hard to produce a future for our children; to rid ourselves of alcohol, tobacco, gambling, laziness and dependency; and to work to make our neighborhoods decent places for us to live. This kind of action on our part could lead to a healthier relationship between the races.

Certainly if we look at our females as that which God produced for us, then we would have to expect the white man to leave our women and girls alone. True love, however, transcends color and race. We must ask the question of those who have gone the way of having interracial relations, is the love a true love, or is it merely an acting out of a corrupted fantasy which is held by both black and white? When we, as a people, are healed of our mental, moral and spiritual sickness, then maybe we can look across racial lines and see the true value and worth of one another. However, healing of the deadly diseases of white supremacy and black inferiority has to take place **first**!

I have to stand and speak for the voiceless, whose leadership has often been quiet or weak in the face of an open enemy. Although I have been misrepresented by the media, here is a new opportunity to receive my message and judge it against the criterion of truth.

Am I really an anti-Semite? Am I really a hater? Can these charges really be proven? When people disagree, the intelligent and rational thing to do is to have a dialogue. Perhaps through dialogue differences can be reconciled. If anything that I have said or written is proved to be a lie, then I will retract my words and apologize before the world.

The Honorable Elijah Muhammad taught us that the way to stop back-biting and slander is to gather the parties together and allow them to present their charges and evidence to each other's face, then we will know where the truth rests and where the lie rests. We are willing to sit and meet before the world and discuss our position. We recognize the ability of the American government and business community to help the black community. The Nation of Islam, in turn, can help America solve its problems. But we cannot solve any problems by bowing down to falsehood.

The Honorable Elijah Muhammad pointed out to us that Babylon, that great and wicked city, could have been healed. She was not healed because she refused to listen to guidance coming to her kings from the mouth of one of her Hebrew slaves. He pointed this out to indicate that America, though dying, can also be healed.

In the design for the original Seal for this country, the pillar of fire in a cloud, expressive of the Divine presence and command - that was also written of in the Bible as seen in a vision by Ezekiel - is now a reality in America. In the Seal's design, the reason that Pharaoh was depicted with a sword in his hand is to symbolize America's pursuit of world dominion by way of skilled machinations backed up by force. America has held a whole nation in captivity for over 400 years - even as Pharaoh did in the biblical history of Moses and the ancient Hebrews - and she has done so by use of force and wicked machinations. The beam of light that was seen shining down on the face of Moses in the design for the original Seal of this country is a sign that the light from God is now beaming down on one from among the ex-slaves. In that light is the guidance that can heal America, the modern Babylon and the modern Egypt. Will America be healed?

A man was born in Georgia and was privileged to meet a Master Teacher, Who gave him the keys for liberating the minds of our people to form the true basis of a new world order. He laid the foundation upon which I stand today. On October 7, 1897, in a little town called Sandersville, Georgia, mother Marie (Poole) Muhammad gave birth to a noble black man who was given a great light by his Teacher, Master Fard Muhammad, so that a light would be lifted up in the midst of gross darkness. That light is the teachings of the Honorable Elijah Muhammad, which I am sharing with America right now.

We have the torchlight. America is being challenged to take the bushel basket off the light. Let us sit down and talk about bringing real solutions before the American people, as civilized people should and are obligated to do.

The Kingdom of God is an egalitarian kingdom structured on truth, where each of us will be treated with fairness and justice. America could become the basis for the Kingdom of God. She has within her borders every nation, kindred and tongue. If they could be made peaceful, productive and mutually respecting, you would have the basis for the Kingdom of God right here on earth.

However, what America does not have is the teaching that would make one people out of the many creeds, colors and nationalities that occupy this land. That teaching cannot be the skilled wisdom from the political leadership that subordinates the language and culture of America's diverse members, while lifting the American way of life as the model - which is very racist and white supremacist in nature. The current American way of life can only produce an apparent unity among caucasians, because it negates the diversity and beauty of the non-white population. You can never achieve unity, or E Pluribus Unum, in this country under the doctrine of white supremacy.

**America needs a spiritual healing.** In the scriptures it reads, *"If my people, which are called by my name, shall humble themselves and pray, and seek my face, and turn from their wicked ways; then will I hear from heaven, and will forgive their sin, and will heal their land."* (II Chronicles 7:14) This is the promise of God for us, and for all of America. Moses and Aaron set two signs before the people, one of life and a blessing, and the other of death and a cursing. He said, *"...choose life, that both thou and thy seed may live."* (Deuteronomy 30:19) The Honorable Elijah Muhammad and Louis Farrakhan say to America the same.

We need to humble ourselves and pray to Allah, God, so that we might receive that same spiritual message that Paul refers to in his words concerning Christ. Paul said, in Christ, *"There is no Jew nor Greek, there is neither bond nor free, there is neither male nor female: for ye are all one in Christ Jesus."* (Galations 3:28) Paul envisioned the end of nationalism, the end of classism and the end of sexism. He envisioned it through the true message of the man called Christ.

Even though America claims to be a Christian country, America, evidently, has missed the message of Christ, or has yet to receive His true message. However, once that true message is given, those who truly want righteousness, justice and peace will gravitate toward that message and they could form the basis of the Kingdom of God on earth. This can be achieved by establishing the truth that frees white people from the sickness of white supremacy and frees black people from the sickness of black inferiority, and lifts us up from an inferior condition and mentality - setting a new standard by which we all should live. The new standard is duty to God and service to our fellow man.

The Honorable Elijah Muhammad taught us that the greatest of all religious principles is to follow the Golden Rule: Do unto others as you would have them do unto you, and love for your brother what you love for yourself.

## Table of Figures

# *Endnotes*

1. *Economic Report of the President*, Transmitted to the Congress February 1992 (Washington, D.C.: U. S. Government Printing Office, 1992), p. 396.

2. *Building a Competitive America*, Competitiveness Policy Council, First Annual Report to the President and Congress (Washington, D.C.: U. S. Government Printing Office, March 1,1992), p. 2.

3. *Ibid.*

4. *Department of Labor, Bureau of Labor Statistics.*

5. *Andrew Hacker, Two Nations: Black and White, Separate, Hostile, Unequal, p. 103.*

6. *Department of Labor, Bureau of Labor Statistics.*

7. *Donald L. Barlett and James B. Steele, America: What Went Wrong?, p. xi.*

8. *Building a Competitive America, p. 1.*

9. *Janet Dewart (ed.), The State of Black America 1991, p. 28 and p. 35.*

10. *Ibid., p.43.*

11. *The Editors of Executive Intelligence Review, Dope, Inc., p. 30.*

12. *President Bush's Fiscal Year 1993 Budget, (Washington, D.C.: U. S. Government Printing Office, 1992), p. 192.*

13. *State and Metropolitan Area Data Book 1991, (Washington, D.C.: U. S. Government Printing Office, 1991), p. 235.*

14. *Harry E. Figgie, Jr. and Gerald J. Swanson, Ph.D., Bankruptcy 1995: The Coming Collapse of America and How to Stop It, p. 53.*

15. *Health, United States, 1990, A Report Prepared by the U.S. Department of Health and Human Services, ( Washington, D.C.: U. S. Government Printing Office, 1991), p. 113.*

16. *Building a Competitive America, p. 20.*

17. *Jonathan Kozol, "Illiterate America," America, (April 11, 1992), pp. 301-303.*

18. *W.E.B. Du Bois, The Souls of Black Folk, pp. 55-56.*

19. *Building a Competitive America, pp. 10-11.*

20. *Hacker, p. 233.*

21. *Economic Report of the President, pp. 386-387.*

22. *Barlett and Steele, p. 7.*

23. *Ross Perot, United We Stand, p. 52.*

24. *Building a Competitive America, p.3*

25. *Du Bois, p. 5.*

26. *Ibid., p. 7.*

27. *Ibid., p. 23.*

28. *Dewart, p. 71.*

29. *Hacker, pp. 85-87.*

30. *"Should Congress Drop Ban on Paying for Abortions?," USA Today, May 24, 1993, p. 11A.*

31. *Alan Ellis, "A Glaring Contrast: Criminal Justice in Black and White," The Wall Street Journal, May 14, 1992, p. A15.*

32. *Du Bois, p. 72.*

33. *Based on data from a Philadelphia study.*

34. *President Bush's Fiscal Year 1993 Budget*, p. 202.

35. *Health, United States, 1990*, p. 192.

36. Jane Heimlich, *What Your Doctor Won't Tell You*, p. 7 and p. 47.

37. *Ibid.*, p. 2.

38. *Ibid.*, p. 75.

39. *Ibid.*, p. 83.

40. *Ibid.*, p. 212.

41. *Ibid.*, p. 92.

42. *Ibid.*, p. 62.

43. The Honorable Elijah Muhammad, *How to Eat to Live: Book One*, pp. 14-15.

44. Jane Heimlich, *What Your Doctor Won't Tell You*, p. 71.

45. *Ibid.*, p. 7.

46. Gaillard Hunt, *The Great Seal of the United States*, pp. 3-4.

47. Du Bois, p. 6.

# Bibliography

Ascher, Carol. "School Programs for African-American Males ... and Females," Phi Delta Kappan, (June, 1992), pp. 777-787.

Barlett, Donald L., and James B. Steele. America What Went Wrong? Kansas City: Andrews and McMeel, 1992.

Brimelow, Peter. "Can Israel go it Alone?," Forbes, (May 11, 1992).

Cantwell Jr., M.D., Alan. AIDS and the Doctors of Death: an Inquiry Into the Origin of the AIDS Epidemic. Los Angeles: Aries Rising Press, 1992.

Clough, Michael. "The United States and Africa: The Policy of Cynical Disengagement," Current History, Vo. 91, No. 565 (May, 1992), pp. 193-198.

Competitiveness Policy Council. Building a Competitive America, First Annual Report to the President & Congress. Washington, D.C.: U.S. Government Printing Office, 1992.

Cross, Theodore. The Black Power Imperative: Racial Inequality and the Politics of Nonviolence. New York: Faulkner Books, 1986.

Dewart, Janet (ed.). The State of Black America. New York: The National Urban League, Inc., 1991.

Donohue, John W. "Lazarus' Schools," America, (April 11, 1992), pp. 301-303.

Du Bois, W.E.B.. The Souls of Black Folk. New York: Bantum Books, 1989.

Economic Report of the President. Transmitted to the
    Congress February 1992. Washington, D.C.: United
    States Government Printing Office, 1992.

The Editors of *Executive Intelligence Review*. Dope, Inc.
    Washington, D.C.: Executive Intelligence Review,
    1992.

Ellis, Alan. "A Glaring Contrast: Criminal Justice in
    Black and White," The Wall Street Journal, May 14,
    1992, p. A15.

Figgie, Jr., Harry E., with Gerald J. Swanson, Ph.D.
    Bankruptcy 1995: The Coming Collapse of America
    and How to Stop It.. Boston: Little, Brown &
    Company, 1992.

Foote, Jr., Cornelius F. "Will U.S. Africa Policy Change?,"
    Black Enterprise, (April, 1992), p.29.

Hacker, Andrew. Two Nations: Black and White,
    Separate, Hostile, Unequal. New York: Charles
    Scribner's Sons, 1992.

Heimlich, Jane. What Your Doctor Won't Tell You. New
    York: HarperCollins Publishers, 1990.

The Holy Bible. Authorized King James Version. Iowa
    Falls: World Bible Publishers, Inc.

The Holy Qur'an. Arabic Text, English Translation and
    Commentary by Maulana Muhammad Ali. Sixth
    Edition. Chicago: Specialty Promotions Co. Inc.,
    1973.

Hunt, Gaillard. The Great Seal of the United States.
    Washington, D.C.: Paul Foster Case, 1935.

Jaynes, Gerald David, and Robin M. Williams, Jr. (eds.).
    A Common Destiny: Blacks and American Society.
    Washington, D.C.: National Academy Press, 1989.

Medved, Michael. <u>Hollywood vs. America: Popular Culture and the War on Traditional Values</u>. New York: HarperCollins, 1992.

Muhammad, The Honorable Elijah. <u>How to Eat to Live: Book One</u>. Chicago: Muhammad's Temple of Islam No. 2, 1967.

National Educational Goals Panel. <u>The National Education Goals Report: Building a Nation of Learners</u>. Washington, D.C.: United States Government Printing Office, 1991.

Perot, Ross. <u>United We Stand</u>. New York: Hyperion, 1992.

<u>President Bush's Fiscal Year 1993 Budget</u>. Washington, D.C.: United States Government Printing Office, 1992.

U.S. Bureau of the Census. <u>State and Metropolitan Area Data Book, 1991: Metropolitan Areas, Central Cities, States</u>. Washington, D.C.: United States Government Printing Office, 1991.

U.S. Bureau of the Census, Current Population Reports, Series P-20, No. 448. <u>The Black Population in the United States: March 1990 and 1989</u>. Washington, D.C.: United States Government Printing Office, 1991.

"World Literacy Rate Rises," <u>The Futurist</u>, (September-October, 1991), p.47.

Wright, Bruce. <u>Black Robes, White Justice: Why our Legal System Doesn't Work for Blacks</u>. New York: Carol Publishing Group, 1987.